Praise for *Bliss Out*

"Every page is sprinkled with decisive insights to turn your bliss into reality."

DANIEL BEAUCHAMP, managing director of Merck Animal Health, France

"A blissful, inspiring book that will change how you approach your day and live your life."

STUART ELLIS-MYERS, CEO of Mental Health for Life

"Like a collaboration between the Dalai Lama and Dolly Parton, we learn about the unexpected interconnectivity of direction, positivity, compassion, belief, wisdom, and success. My advice to you: Read *Bliss Out*, and in the words of Bob Marley, get ready to 'Be Happy.'"

MARK DEVOLDER, change management speaker

"*Bliss Out* is a must-read for everyone who wants to take their life to the next and higher level of meaning and happiness."

BRIAN LEE, CSP, HoF, CEO and founder of Custom Learning Systems

"Time flew by while reading *Bliss Out*! I found my bliss in these pages. Hustle doesn't drive my life—inspiration does."

BRENDA MORGAN, senior manager at Walmart

Bliss
Out

Bliss Out

Feel-Good Habits to Lift Your Hustle Hangover

JODY URQUHART

PAGE TWO

Cataloguing in publication information is
available from Library and Archives Canada.
ISBN 978-1-77458-108-7 (paperback)
ISBN 978-1-77458-109-4 (ebook)

Page Two
pagetwo.com

Edited by Kendra Ward
Copyedited by Rachel Ironstone
Cover and interior design by Taysia Louie

idoinspire.com

This book is dedicated to my son,
Branden Urquhart, and to my partner,
Don Ward, who inspire me every
day with their wisdom, kindness,
and ability to laugh at life.

Contents

Introduction
Bliss Is Waiting for You

YEARS AGO I participated in a seven-day personal development seminar on happiness. The course attracted a diverse group of people keen to discover a better way of life. Not that the current life of any one of them was that terrible, but clearly we all longed for more. There were lawyers, caregivers, moms, even dog walkers—people of all ages collecting together to understand our elusive happiness.

We spent the first five days deeply dissecting our negative emotions. We each told stories of our past that brought up anger, fear, and resentment. Some people's stories were really tragic. We were working through heavy stuff, and it was draining.

By the end of day five, we were strung out and exhausted, and a few people had quit the course.

Thankfully, in the last two days, we started to explore positive thoughts and feelings. We talked about happiness, hope, optimism, and love. The energy lifted. People laughed and looked a lot more content. A couple even fell in love there and went on to marry.

The turnaround was dramatic. What's interesting to me is that our lives hadn't changed for the better, yet, but we were definitely happier, making it pretty clear: the focus on happiness made us happier. Go figure.

I wondered why, in a happiness course, we didn't spend *more* time focused on happiness.

Because I'm a motivational speaker and personal improvement junkie, over the years I've found myself in front of a lot of psychologists and therapists. Yet I don't often find digging into memories of tragedy, anger, and fear helpful; rarely does reliving the past move a person forward.

Dissecting why bad things happened, who's to blame, and how it impacted you is always messy and complicated. It activates negative thoughts and feelings about the past, and they become your point of attraction. The more you return to these thoughts, the more they build negative momentum, and the more they can hold you back. You become compelled toward more thoughts of agony and resentment.

Some negative topics become so energized that they produce a toxic chemical cocktail in your body. Thinking about them generates something like a hangover, and when you keep indulging in these topics, they make you feel worse.

At some point, we all hunger to move forward. When everyone around us is compelled to brood over excess workloads, conflict, and uncertainty, we feel drained and stuck. We want to cling to hope, progress, and opportunity to progress and feel better. In the midst of stress, any positive emotion like joy, appreciation, or fun would give us tremendous, immediate relief. Complaining makes us feel bad, and it never helps us move forward. We long for purpose, passion, and a steady stream of hope and eagerness for a future that matters. We want to make a difference instead of being stuck giving purpose to problems.

Yet, for some reason, even self-improvement heroes focus on what's wrong with our lives instead of what's right. Conflict gets way too much stage time in society today. We're too heavily concentrated on our differences. And it's holding us all back.

Focusing on what's wrong with you (or your life) builds up a case for more misery. Focusing on gratitude, joy, compassion, hope, optimism, and all positive feelings moves you forward. Life becomes much easier when you fixate on happiness.

This book is about feeling good. Consider it an all-out advocate for your good vibes. In the pages ahead, I will continually nudge you forward, toward blissed-out good feelings. I'm not saying suck it up and pretend everything is okay. I discourage you from ignoring or suppressing hard feelings. But you will learn to use positive emotions like kindness and self-compassion to wiggle forward and feel better. The "feel-good habits section" I include at the end of each chapter will guide you to a better-feeling place.

For now, just know that you don't have to work for happiness—you already have it. It's not something you hustle after; blissing out in happiness is a state of being. This book is designed to help you live up to the prosperity, happiness, love, and joy you desire.

Doesn't this sound great? As chaos and stress consume everyone around you, you can rely on your good vibes to stay calm and focused. You can bliss out, soak up the present moment, see potential instead of stress. In this feel-good state of being, you will accomplish everything you want with clarity.

Life is not meant to be a chore but an adventure in happiness. With today's excessive workloads, happiness usually takes a back seat. I want to bring this positive emotion to the forefront of everything you do and show you how your good vibes propel your life forward.

I'm captivated by happiness, why some people have it but so many people don't. I've read many books on the topic, most written by scientists and psychologists trying to dissect this elusive thing called joy. I'm so grateful for their rigorous approach, and all the research suggests one thing: happiness is good for you. We all want more of it.

So many people have tried to crush happiness, including me. I want to feel better, after all. But my deep-down sense is that feeling good should be easy. Maybe all this analyzing just complicates everything.

Through my own quest for happiness I've stumbled across one glaring insight: happiness is not a goal, it's a feeling. It's not a quest, it's something we all have available, right now. Every time we look for it outside ourselves, we place conditions on finding it. But that's looking in the wrong direction. Because happiness is inside us.

What is a hustle hangover?

Have you ever had a hangover before? When you wake up in the morning and realize you drank too much alcohol? And now you can't find your phone or your self-respect? Your body feels exhausted, you're worn out, and you can't think clearly. Your hangover is your body saying, *Let's not do that too often, okay?* Those of us who learn from the hangover will listen.

But what about the hangover that stress, conflict at work, and otherwise struggling against life gives you? Have you noticed how the longer you think about stressful circumstances, the worse you feel? The more you try to push problems away, the more irritable you get? Your body and mind feel exhausted, worn out, and maybe you can't think clearly...

That's a hustle hangover.

And the kicker is, this hangover doesn't go away after a bottle of Gatorade and a good night's sleep (although a good night's sleep never hurt anything). As long as that stress keeps showing up in your life and triggering you, you will feel it hanging over your head from one day to the next.

The cure to this hangover is to bliss out. Stop thinking about those stressful circumstances and use good feelings to create clarity and move forward. Just like you stop reaching for another drink, you stop reaching for those toxic thoughts. Instead, you climb into the present moment and locate joy, happiness, and all the feel-good feelings precisely where they are patiently waiting—inside you. Bliss out on these good vibes and you will sustain a higher vibration that will last.

Hey, hustler, keep it simple!

Are you ambitious but somehow feeling frustrated and stuck? Stuck in your career, stuck in your relationship, or stuck in any area of your life? But would you like to feel good no matter what? Would you like things to move forward for you with more ease? Do joy, meaning, and purpose sound like fun? If so, this book is for you. You're going to learn some simple feel-good habits that turn your focus from the inside out, to create a life that's fulfilling.

When you take all the personality and feeling out of work and relationships, all you're left with is effort and force, pushing your agenda forward regardless of the human impact. Taken to the extreme, a hustler can be seen as aggressive and unethical.

Many organizations prioritize effort and results, sometimes at the expense of people.

Feeling like you have to keep pumping out effort to show progress equates to success by sacrifice. To give more time to work, we sideswipe good feelings and neglect relationships. This hangover is driven by too much emphasis on the hard part of our work, causing us to squeeze out passion.

The remedy is feeling good. Hope, optimism, joy, compassion, purpose, and passion to the rescue! These uplifting thoughts and feelings propel you forward without struggle and sacrifice. You can do the same amount of work (and more!)

while feeling inspired, enthusiastic, understanding, and upbeat. Surprisingly innovative solutions spring up and give life to your job while your carefree, optimistic attitude teases away stress.

Keep it simple. Choose joy, not stress.

When we are stuck, our world doesn't look favorable to us, and we feel irritated. Circumstances in our jobs, relationships, or the economy make us feel jilted and pick up a strong backward momentum that can end up stalling our lives. Our goal is to feel good; but life makes us feel bad.

But we're going to flip the focus.

Through some fun and easy activities, you will learn how your thoughts and feelings matter more than anything else. You will learn to focus on your inner world and nurture love, gratitude, prosperity, hope, and joy regardless of what's happening in your life. You will use positive thoughts and feelings and their forward momentum to climb out of challenging emotions and into living your life. No matter how messed up your life may seem, it can reveal joy. This book is designed to show you how perpetual positive thoughts and emotions will move you in the direction of your goals, faster and with playfulness and ease. Because happiness is not a goal, anytime you place goals or conditions on it, it will hide.

This adventure is held together by principles of the laws of attraction and mindfulness. You will learn how to use the law of attraction and elevate your thoughts and emotions above the fear, stress, and emotions that drag you down. You will consistently lift upward, using mindfulness to appreciate life.

What is elevating?

Whenever I talk about *elevating*, I simply mean to turn your focus inward and bliss out on good feelings. Despite your boss's heavy demands on you or cranky customers screaming for your attention, you can look inside yourself and bliss out in calm and joy. Then you can smother that difficult world with ease and potential. You'll get the job done without a hitch and feel good while you do it.

Everything in the universe is composed of energy that vibrates. Including you. Right now, an energy is moving through every cell of your body. All thoughts have their own vibrational frequency. In these pages, you will learn to bliss out, which means to bring uplifting thoughts and feelings into your brain and body in the present moment. These gestures mean so much. Uplifting thoughts allow positive feelings to flourish and build a momentum that gives your life direction. It broadens your perspective and shows you opportunity instead of stress.

Through the ideas in this book, you will be tapping into universal principles. There are universal laws that say what you focus on expands. Focus on negative things and, like a magnet, you attract more stress and upheaval. Believe in your potential and with a sustained effort you will invite positive things into your life. Bombard your mind and body with dreams of prosperity, once you remove barriers of doubt, and your own belief in those dreams makes you unstoppable.

Dancing through this text are principles of mindfulness as well. Whenever you practice bringing your attention to the present moment, you are being mindful. Mindfulness is the awareness that emerges when you learn to pay attention to things as they actually are.[1] It allows you to see the world directly, not through a lens of fear, judgment, and doubt. The ability to be in the present moment has scientifically been proven to have many benefits, including reduced stress, increased focus, boosted creativity, and a calm sympathetic nervous system.

When you are in the moment, pure positive vibrational energy can flow through you. It's not tripped up by fear or doubt. When you sit still and calm your thoughts, you can catch this vibrational force moving through you. You feel a state of bliss.

Your life, on your terms

You are going to discover how to elevate your vibration, inspire hope, and attract the life you deserve. On your own terms.

This book is designed to activate hope and positive emotion inside you. Don't give way to the temptation to passively read it. Don't pound through the pages like it's something to conquer on your to-do list. Instead, soak it up. Let positive emotions vibrate inside you and let them flourish in your subconscious. I have actively used repetition to pepper your inner being with hope. I want you to feel these words, to bliss out on them. If words provoke you, read them again and again. Feel energy swell inside you and crowd out the doubt and pessimistic thoughts that try to stifle your brilliance.

What lies beneath the rubble of broken dreams is potential. Once you remove the barriers that stress and fear place on you, you no longer have a jilted relationship to your life. Getting to your destination is much easier when you stop tripping yourself up with doubt. Underneath all the awkwardness stress places on you is potential. Having left behind worry and doubt, you can move more quickly toward the life you want.

1

CLIMB INTO LIFE

GET YOUR
DIRECTION RIGHT

HAPPINESS IS *not a goal, it's a feeling. It's not something you have to work for, it's something you have.* This simple statement can transform your life.

Most things in life require effort and hustle, but not positive feelings. They are inside you right now and ready to blossom anytime you give them attention. Good feelings will always direct you toward your potential.

Prioritizing effort makes stress your focal point. Choose passion instead.

Bliss out—it only takes seventeen seconds

To bliss out is to sustain a feel-good, high-vibration energy inside you. You reach this state by practicing the feel-good habits as described in the pages ahead.

To bliss out means you reach a feeling of euphoria and sustain it. You let go of all negativity, tension, and pressure and be in happiness, absorbed in the present moment. Sustaining blissed-out feelings imprints the uplifting vibration in your body, which makes it easier to return to.

According to the work of Abraham Hicks, when you hold a thought for seventeen seconds, you ignite its vibration.[2] The longer you hold that vibration, the more powerful it becomes. It attracts more vigorous, uplifting thoughts and vibrations. So, to bliss out, you need to hold the thought-vibration for at least seventeen seconds. Once you reach a blissful state, it will be much easier to stay in it. In the moment, this powerful vibration will draw more uplifting energy to you.

When you bliss out, you are in your most calm and focused state. Bliss doesn't make you flaky or unrealistic, it means you *appreciate* stress and see potential.

Blissing out is the practice of invoking a feel-good vibration that, over time, becomes a reliable force that propels you forward.

Don't equate blissing out to ignoring reality. Instead, it's a heightened state of attention that allows you to accept reality and deal with everything with more clarity. A practiced state of feeling good will help you stay focused and calm, especially when life demands a lot.

Blissing out is a feel-good state of being that does not require you to hustle. You don't have to work for these feelings.

Why do we hustle?

These days, we all have more work to do and fewer resources. This trend doesn't seem to be going away.

So what are our options? We just have to work harder. Naturally, we'll have to cut into family and leisure time and give that time to work. The job must get done. Less joy, less fun, more busy-ness.

We've all grudgingly turned our back on enjoyment because duty calls. But all this work is making us feel bad. When work always hangs over us, we feel burnt out. How is that productive?

Here's how it feels for me: All this excessive work strangles me with worry, doubt, and uncertainty, even when I'm not working. As I chase these thoughts around, I'm basically pouring an adrenaline and cortisol cocktail. That's hard on my body. Over time, I start to feel hungover from all this work and all these stress hormones. That work keeps hounding me—and this hangover never subsides.

Workloads rarely let up, and there will always be more to do; this may never change. However, the tragic struggle we entertain around all types of effort can change—and it should. We were hired to be hardworking, but if that's a hassle, it is on us.

Move forward and feel good

In the pages ahead, you will learn to let go of the struggle pegged around all your effort, and you will move forward and feel good.

This is not about being lazy; it's about potential. When you can renew hope, optimism, and passion in all areas of your life, even when life is overwhelming, you will be propelled forward. This is not about challenging workloads, efficiency, or demanding a more balanced schedule. Instead you give up the inner struggle around outer priorities and feel good while you accomplish everything you want.

Happy and productive

Hustle is about productivity. It's about results, accomplishments, and pushing your agenda. Most work environments revolve around the hustle.

In this environment, happiness is often given the cold shoulder because we think of it as a side benefit. It's something we

Ignorance **is not bliss.**

have to earn. Once I've crushed my goals, I'll be happy. Once I've finished my work, I can have fun. However, this is not an either/or situation. We don't have to barter one for the other. You can have the hustle and happiness *at the same time*.

Happiness is not an effort. It's not something that you work for, it's something you have. Right now. It's this amazing internal force and energy inside you, and if you pay attention to it, it will bring you to the life you want. Joy and bliss is not a doing, it's a feeling. You can be happy and work, you can be content and exercise, you can be elated and do anything at all. And you should, because this internal inferno of happiness will fill you with delight while you get everything that you desire.

The reason work is tragic for most people is that their direction is messed up. They are led by a hustle, focused on crushing their to-do list. Joy, passion, and potential are an afterthought. If they flipped this focus, they would have more fun and bolt toward their potential. Discovering that good feelings make everything easier is glorious.

Anytime you feel bad, it's a signal that your direction is off. You've put hustle before happiness and it's holding you back. If, instead, you think about what you want and feel good about it, you can't go wrong. Bliss out on feelings of success and you naturally propel yourself forward.

Joy buzz

I roll out of bed feeling excited about the day. Joyful happiness seems to be buzzing through me. I feel uplifted and powerful. The joy seems to spread—not in a practiced way, as in the routine of applying peanut butter to bread, but in an expansive current that radiates through me. It's as though I flipped a light switch with my positive emotions, and the current just flows through me.

I reach for my cell phone. The content of a text message draws me into a conflict between my tenant and my property manager. They are both angry, and I've suddenly become the referee trying to direct the situation. Anger craves resolution: someone has to be right, and someone has to be wrong. But I don't call the shots anyway, so I wonder why I'm even involved.

All I know is that they've ruined my vibe. That flowing, uplifting buzz I was blissing out on is gone, replaced by aggravation. This heavy feeling doesn't flow. It sinks. It sits in my belly and drags me down.

Annoyance has stifled my energy and has the potential to ruin my day. It all depends on how many other people line up to throw off my balance with their endless demands. I can't loosen up the anchor in my belly and feel good unless I'm free of these hassles.

Or can I? Don't some irritating people tell us that happiness comes from within?

Yes, they do. And years ago, I decided to believe them. I've learned that the joyful bliss buzz is real, and it's far more powerful than my tragic to-do list. As long as I believe in the happy currents, they can transform any misery into opportunity and potential.

I want you to know this potential too. It's life-changing. I'd love for you to believe in the power of your own blissful positive vibes and use this mighty energy to live your life from the inside out.

Inside you is a strong positive force that is fueled by your focus and belief in it.

You can feel engaged, positive, focused, and happy. This vivacious spring in your step is no accident; it is an energy vibe that builds positive momentum into your life. It's reliable and uncontainable. It wants nothing from you but for you to feel good.

Happiness asks only one thing of you: to bliss out on it more often.

I want these words to lift off this page into your being. Let the positive energy spread through you and all over your life. I want you to spew positive vibration, from inside you out, all over everything that happens to you, good or bad.

Getting your direction right

The direction of this adventure is always forward into your life, and it will always feel good. Think about what it feels like to move forward. Doesn't it feel good when you complete a task? When you go on a journey or on a date, run a marathon, learn to cook, finish on budget, or get a promotion. You are moving forward each time, and you know because it feels good.

Nobody likes to be stuck. Everyone wants to move forward, and to do that means you should always look where you're going, not where you are. Keep asking yourself what you want and where you're headed, and be mindful of that direction.

Anytime you don't feel good, you know you're headed in the wrong direction.

Yes, this means your feelings matter. They are your guide. Most people don't understand their feelings. As a whole, emotions seem complicated and messy. There are lots of them, from anger to sadness, to contentment, to joy. (At least one scientific study shows there are likely twenty-seven or more emotions.[3]) Relax. No one here is going to ask you to analyze them.

This won't be a complicated endeavor because emotions go in one of only two directions. Up or down. This is all you need to know: do you feel good or bad? You don't need a therapist to tell you if you feel happy or sad. You always know. Every time you feel good, your life moves forward. Every time you feel bad, you hold yourself back. This is why positive thoughts and feelings are key to your potential. They pull you toward what you want, and as long as fear or doubt doesn't get in the way, you get there.

On this adventure, your only destination is the present moment—being mindful of how you feel right now. It's like driving around with no road map. How do you set a direction if you don't have a physical destination? Your emotions guide the way. Feeling good is like stepping on the accelerator in your car. You move forward. Feeling bad is like putting on the brakes. It's holding you back. If you focus on what you're feeling inside as a compass for guidance, you will always know which direction you are headed. And anytime your outside world disrupts your inside happiness, you know you're headed in the wrong one. You've got to reorient yourself to set a forward course once again.

Occasionally taking time in your day to bliss out on positive thoughts and feelings will create an uplifting vibration that will become a sustaining force. It will make your whole life easier.

Conditions trip you up

In college my friend Maura pulled me aside before I was about to give a big speech and said, "I love you, but you look a bit pale."

I instantly started questioning myself. Is my lipstick too bright? Should I have chosen a different blouse? Maura always looks great. Meeting her standards is hard. All I knew was I had been feeling good, but suddenly I was uneasy and my mind was all messed up.

"I love you, but . . ." These words are like a loaded gun. The *love* part sounds great, but what comes after hangs around our necks like a noose.

Love is a beautiful thing that we could easily bliss out on, but it gets complicated when we muddy it with conditions.

Love feels good. The conditions we place on it do not. Whenever you need to meet a condition (say, to look good, be promoted, complete a task, or catch a break) for life to work out in your favor and for you to feel happy, you are headed in the wrong direction. The condition is like a broken GPS telling you to go in reverse.

Change your direction: remember, happiness is inside you and it's ready to take you forward, no matter what the state of your life. All you have to do is release the thought (the condition) and focus on happiness. You don't need to hustle for joy, you already have it. It's inside you. Just change your direction, focus from the inside out on that joy, and it will flourish.

Here's an example that most ambitious, caring parents can probably relate to. When my son was five, he got lost in IKEA. I looked for two hours and finally found him hiding under a bed display. He heard me calling but wanted me to find him. More and more lately, I've noticed he's developing his own personality and not listening to me. Every day he's becoming more independent, and I can't protect him from this great big world anymore. Sometimes I wish I could shove him back up inside my uterus. He's safer there.

Parents always want the best for their kids and usually think they know what's best. In these relationships, mixing up your inside good feelings of love and joy for your children with your outside conditions designed to help and protect them is all too easy:

- I'll be happy if you just listen and do what I say.
- I'll be happy if you stop picking on your brother.
- I'll be happy if you become an attorney.

We love our kids no matter what, but we don't realize we're placing all these complicated conditions on our love and happiness. With each condition, we complicate the relationship.

Your attention to unwanted conditions always holds them in your life. Focus on anyone's deficiencies and, in the moment, your feelings about the flaws become stronger than your love.

Worry about your kids, and you grow your fear and worry instead of your trust and love. The longer you think about anything, the stickier it becomes as it attracts more like it into your life. Focus on the unconditional love you have for someone and your relationship will always grow.

Unconditional love is just that: a boundless blissful feeling inside you that can spread to all areas of your life, regardless of the conditions.

When life looks unfavorable to you, you start to feel bad. Now, your circumstances are reminding you to remove the conditions you keep placing on joy. Because happiness is a feeling, it cannot be boxed in by your goals. You just need to take your eyes off your disappointing conditions and look at where you're going and the joy you want, not where you're at.

This feels confusing because our world is full of conditions. We apply rules, guidelines, and goals to everything. We put them on ourselves, our lives, and our loved ones. Rules aren't bad; they can provide clarity and direction. But we make ourselves miserable by applying rules to our good feelings.

"I'll be happy if you change" is where the real confusion sets in.

Most people's love isn't free. It has to be earned. When you expect people to earn your love, you place a bounty on a powerful, positive force that would transform your life if you let it.

Real love, joy, and appreciation come freely, without conditions. They are inside you and they are boundless. Nobody has to do anything for you, or to you, for you to be happy.

It's so rewarding to be kind to others because you genuinely care about them. Not out of guilt or because of a court order.

I have a sign in my office that says, *Use your smile to change the world, but don't let the world change your smile.* Simple, profound, and true. If you can believe in the beautiful happiness inside you and not let the world around you dampen its spirit, you will find joy and potential. You don't have to search to find joy, you are not on a treasure hunt for happiness and bliss. It's inside you right now. Just let go of the conditions.

The world outside you will never deliver happiness. But that blissful feeling within can take you screaming (with joy!) toward your potential.

When life is a struggle

For years I struggled with anxiety. Green smoothies, cognitive therapy, and expensive life coaches promised me relief. I clung to the false hopes they instilled. Yet anxiety built. It sneered at me as if to say, *Nice try*. Stalking solutions to my problems on Google made me feel even worse.

The endless scavenger hunt outside myself for a mysterious solution was probing in the wrong direction. Poking around in my life was irritating my calm. The hunt for a remedy to anxiety was taking me further from resolve because it was taking me further from myself. As I scoured the vitamin aisle for answers, my emotions were fired up and reinforced my fear that something was terribly wrong with me. I labeled myself as anxious, and increased my inventory of apprehension.

Finally, I flipped my focus from external distractions and discovered feelings of calm are within me, not on the supermarket check-out stand. I had searched for solutions for over a decade, and once I focused on calm inside, it took me three days to relieve my anxiety. To get your direction right, always focus on what you want (for instance, health, wealth, happiness) instead of what you don't want (stress, anxiety, or poor health).

My intention is to flagrantly promote your good feelings. I want to stir up the happiness and passion that I know exists inside you. But what if, like me at that time, you don't feel good? What if life sucks? Should you ignore that and pretend everything's okay? No. This is not about repressing negative feelings. In fact, we will use compassion to ease our way into better feelings.

As long as you focus on what you want and where you're headed, you are always moving forward, and you will always feel better. Muster all your energy to shift your focus to happiness, love, joy, optimism, forgiveness, kindness, or feelings of success. Anytime you wallow in fear or doubt, distress over your mistakes, worry about others, or try to assess blame, you move away from your life.

When you can tap into your good feelings inside you (and don't worry, you will do just that), you catapult yourself into a vibrant day. When you feel bad, the outside conditions of your world (your job, your divorce, your tax return) hold you back in fear and doubt.

The simple mental habits we unravel in this book will continually guide you forward. A great reward to cherish is that feeling good is easy and fun. If it doesn't feel that way, you're likely complicating it with fear and doubt.

When tenants, property managers, children, spouses, or bosses annoy you, you are putting outside conditions on your inside happiness. You need them to change for you to be happy. If you wake up in the morning and say, "I will be happy as long as all my conditions are met," happiness is impossible.

Unhappy emotions that anchor you in misery are a signal to remove the conditions. They are a signal that you are not living your life from the inside out but the other way around. Your direction is off, and you're letting the current conditions of your life dictate your happiness.

You simply can't bliss out and stress out at the same time.

Your thoughts and emotions are invisible, so they are often dismissed, yet they are your most powerful force. Live your life from the inside out by believing in the power of your thoughts

If you think about what you want and feel good about it, **you can't go wrong.**

and feelings to transform your life. Focus less on the trappings of the world around you and more on the emotional vibration inside you. Feel good now.

Joy of the journey

If your attention is heavily focused on achieving outcomes, you miss the splendid journey along the way to reaching your destination. You will be tempted to scale back any relaxing, expansive, playful detours in reaching your goal. Cut out all the frivolous perks, and get where you want to go faster and more efficiently.

Let's lift your hustle. I want you to cherish all the joy you can out of your journey and let wonderful outcomes just flow into your life as a result of your good feelings.

For a moment, consider planning a vacation. Imagine getting on a plane, checking into a hotel, and sitting by the pool drinking margaritas while soaking up the sun. When your vacation is over, you get back on a plane and ultimately end up right back where you started. At home. In other words, you're already at your final destination—so you can skip the vacation.

You would never think that way, right? Why? Because you intuitively recognize value in the joy along the journey. The only outcome of this trip is pure pleasure. This innate satisfaction is not a goal, it is a feeling.

Your whole life is this journey. To get the most out of it, focus less on your destination, goals, and outcomes and more on your direction. That direction is to always move forward with good feelings as your guide. Now you can relish the joy of the journey of life and get everything you desire, without the struggle.

How did it get so complicated?

It can't help itself. Your life is complicated. And when you focus on its endless ups and downs instead of on your joy, it gets sticky. When you glare at your life and expect it to perform the way you want, it won't. Instead, stress, moodiness, fear, and resentment cling to you like Velcro. Inside and out.

Does this sound like you?

Your day is tied to continually fighting problems, and you find more hurdles waiting for you around every corner. Other people's priorities follow you around like a nasty odor. Sometimes you wonder what the significance of this life really is. You work hard but feel like you were meant for more.

Your job likely places ambitious conditions on you all day long. Your work ethic and hustle may be assigning prerequisites to your potential, holding you back. Your drive to be the best for others has always motivated you. It's also the proper thing to do. Because you're ambitious, you'd never aim to be average. You won't be an average parent, an average employee, an average leader, or an average spouse. For you, being average is an insult.

People also rely on you; you work hard, and you're proud of it. You are indebted to your drive to improve. Some people secretly feel entitled to your dedication, rigorous work ethic, and hustle. Take a small step back and you realize that people chase you around all day with their problems. They need you to faithfully lean in and settle the stress that triggers them. For now.

Curiously, nobody ever calls you to celebrate reports you file or the budget you balanced. It's a continuous cycle of settling setbacks. Progress is a non-event. Problems are a priority.

Are you making problems your priority? Then you're focused on what you don't want instead of on what you yearn for. You are choosing stress over bliss.

When do you appreciate what you have? This same persistent fixer routine appears in your life at home and at work. It has permeated your whole life. But how can that be? Your co-workers and your family are not perpetuating this cycle of worry that has you pouncing on problems. You are.

Your drive to fix everything means life, in all its inherent messiness, is not good enough as it is. Letting unsettling glitches exist means settling for average. And you won't have it.

You may have a laser focus on the obstacles you face. Your desire to fix your life means you constantly battle with the belief that it doesn't work. To appreciate a life that gets your attention only when it is presented as a problem? That is hard. When you predominantly focus on obstacles, the necessary effort to fix them, and the conditions in your way, you stifle the flow of your bliss. You lose touch with your inner joy as you grasp tightly to your outward hustle—like a dog on a leash, your problems lead you through your day.

You can easily reverse the momentum. Instead of shaking down your life looking to fix problems, flip your focus and resolve to feel good often. Diligently throw positive thought and emotions and understanding at everything and everyone around you—especially if they make you feel bad. Let invisible energy wrapped around these thoughts and feelings penetrate and soften your world as you start to build positive momentum. This is a simple mental habit where you diligently focus on where you're headed: toward joy, progress, and potential.

With enough positive feeling, you can really bliss out on your good vibes. And you should because with these zestful feelings you will bolt toward success and potential.

I'd like your potential to leap off these pages at you. Once you realize how much stress is doing a number on you and holding up your journey, you can escape this routine and flow with your passion instead of against it.

When you get your direction right, you move forward and feel good. You naturally focus less on problems of the past and more on solutions in the present that improve the future. You start moving forward, and your good vibes guide you.

Along the way you'll realize your goals are not a problem. But how you might cling to them is. On your quest to conquer goals, you become heavily focused on problems and stress. But behind all goals is a desire to move forward. Joy can spring out of you and transform your life.

Here is another example of a simple forward-moving perspective shift.

I recently spoke at a Zoom event. The speaker before me talked about setting personal boundaries. She was well-spoken and her presentation well researched. Listening to her, I sensed that placing barriers on how people are allowed to treat you can become very complicated. It would be a lot more rewarding to focus on people's positive qualities and how you want to be treated than tearing apart and highlighting how you don't care to be treated. Simply focus on what you want, and you move forward.

Saying no creates limits, and saying yes means more opportunity. Obviously, you aren't going to say yes to everything. Just remember to line up with your decisions. Don't say yes out of guilt, worry, or doubt. Say yes because you want to strengthen your relationship. Say yes because you imagine it will be a fun experience. Say yes because you are keen to learn something new.

Flip your focus

Right here and now, I want you to change the direction of any negative momentum. I want to lure you inside, toward your emotions. Any thoughts and emotional energy you put toward hustling are draining you. Let's lift those conditions.

Flip your focus. This can be simple. If your outside world is irritating your inside world, your job, hard-work ethic, and toughness routine may be creating inner upheaval. As long as your attention is on external circumstances happening in your favor, you will just continue to be irritated.

Joy is not a goal, it's a feeling. Inside you. It won't be manipulated by your priorities.

Believe in feeling good. At work. At home. Anywhere. Pure positive belief in feeling good can turn your momentum around. For the better.

I'm suggesting you live your life from the inside out. It involves a lot of positive intention and belief. The truth is, lots of great things happen in your life every day, but they are glossed over by the need to conquer another dilemma. You skim over joy in favor of stress.

Instead, bliss out: Smother joy and positive thoughts and feelings all over everything that happens to you, and your energy and vibrational momentum will change. The positive emotion will move you forward. And you'll still conquer your goals.

Reading these words, you may sense your work ethic corralling your stress cycle, resisting. Relax. You will not give up on your to-do list. This is not what you're up to. Instead you are climbing out of the false effort that traps you in worry and climbing into the life you want. You are claiming the life you have. And it's more delicious than you realize.

Fear, worry, or doubt always hold you back, questioning the past. Stressing out takes you out of the present moment, while blissing out brings you back to the here and now.

Let's consider a scenario that shows how this works. Shari, for example, had a new colleague that she took an almost instant dislike to. Her thoughts started to muddy because she was spending a lot of time thinking about his past misdeeds. She reminisced about how this new colleague grabbed the spotlight at last week's meeting, taking credit for all her hard work. I get how that would be very annoying for Shari, but that maddening feeling held her back. Literally. In her thoughts she relived the past (last week's meeting) instead of living the amazing life in front of her. Her fuming repetition of the meeting also made her feel bad.

From there, she started skimming over the present moment and jetting into the future. She began fantasizing about how his maneuvers might jeopardize the promotion that she knew she deserved. She planned an exit strategy contingent on whether things improved. Now, where was Shari's joy and happiness? She had one foot in the past and one foot in the future, and she was missing the present moment.

She could choose to focus on the life happening in the here and now in front of her—her great job and how her skills had evolved, or something simpler like the birds chirping outside her window, the gentle spring sun calling up the crocuses, and the pleasant warmth of the tea in her mug. But no! She was missing out. Joy only springs forward in the present moment.

Shari could simplify her whole situation by reminding herself to feel good, often, and by letting that positive emotion spread all over her current situation. Shari built some negative momentum toward her colleague, when instead she could cast understanding and appreciative thoughts and emotions at the irritating new guy to avoid stalling her positive momentum. She could stop labeling him as irritating—knowing everything in life becomes more like the label we give it. Shari could imagine influencing him with her massive inner passion—instead of with chloroform and a rope.

Shari could decide that her new colleague is doing the best he can, that he is probably nervous about his new role. He did not mean to take credit for her work. In fact, it would be good to collaborate with him on this project. They could help each other out and that would benefit everybody.

This positive thought direction could make Shari feel better, progress in her job, and build a better relationship with her colleague. That's forward movement. If Shari can lift and release some of her doubt about her colleague, she might even perpetuate some great thoughts and feelings about her work. Eventually she will bliss out on good feelings like pride and passion for her job. In this elevated state, new ideas will emerge.

When you have one foot in the past and one foot in the future, you are missing the most important moment of all—the present. You're missing out on the joy of the journey.

Stress doesn't have to dig its claws in you when your life butts up against uncertainty. Instead passion and joy can hint you toward potential.

Welcome to the present moment and your real life

Be. Here. Now. Why is that so hard? Why do we continually choose fear and worry over being in the now? The simple answer is that this habit helps us survive. Stress lures you into fear and doubt so that you don't make mistakes, put yourself in danger, or make a fool of yourself.

It's preserving your status quo.

A base level of anxiety, stress, and unhappiness may be your norm. This tendency to get sucked into the past and worry about the future may leave you perpetually worn out as you waste energy needed to live your best life.

Being in the present moment, or the *here and now*, means that you are aware and mindful of what is happening at this very moment. You are not distracted by ruminations about the past or worries about the future but are centered in the now. Your attention is focused on the present moment. Anytime you bliss out on happiness, you are in the here and now; it's your most focused, vibrant state.

Positive thinking and feeling habits can get you there.

As long as your attention is focused on positives—appreciation, love, and joy—you are moving toward the here and now. You are appreciating life right in front of you. You are lifting conditions and relieving resistance to that life. Skim over negativity and focus on building momentum through habits of perpetual positive thoughts and feelings. Eventually you will let go of stress and just be in bliss.

Negativity and conflict get way too much stage time in our world, and positivity has the power to catapult us all forward.

Every time you get tangled up in fear, negativity, worry, or doubt, you wrestle with these emotions. Your thoughts will transport you to the past or a negatively tainted future. All negative emotion keeps you stuck. Rooting around in your past and analyzing tragic memories is rarely helpful. Doubting yourself is not helpful. You can spend your entire life wondering why bad things happen to you, or you can use positive feelings to move forward. Appreciate the past for the lessons it brought you and get on with your amazing life.

Climb into the life you want

Every time you choose gratitude, happiness, or any uplifting vibe, a feel-good habit climbs into your life. These carefree feelings guide you into the present moment, where you can enjoy life.

You hold great power. You can be happy, successful, and stress-free. This exact life is right in front of you. What are you waiting for?

Always look where you are going, **not where you're at.**

The life you have is exactly the one you've been asking for. Maybe it's messy, difficult, and stressful. And you designed it that way. Why would you do that? Because you keep telling yourself about your fears and what you don't want, instead of what you desire.

Your brain is simply giving you what you asked it for. Of course, you want to be energetic and healthy, but instead you keep repeating a narrative about your sore hips and bad back. And they keep getting worse. You actually want meaningful and rewarding work, but instead you keep complaining about excessive workloads. And the work never lets up. You want financial freedom. Instead you struggle to pay the bills and worry about being short on cash. And what does your life give you? Less money. That's what you keep asking it for.

The good news is the brain can change. It's constantly organizing itself. It forms new connections between neurons whenever you learn something new. You can teach your brain to be positive, just by introducing more positive thoughts. Use this positive energy to move forward.

As the years go by and time slaps age on our faces and bodies, many people become more cautious and resist change. But only our thoughts hold us back. Perhaps that's a large and diverse collection of negative thoughts that tie us to the many years we've been alive.

This new direction will cause your inner world to shed resistance, and you will take on the curiosity of a young child. Everything becomes new and exciting. This adventure is rewarding at any age because you learn to appreciate everything. Your life will sparkle with a new tinge of positive appreciation. Nothing will be taken for granted.

Know that what you want wants you. What you give your attention to amplifies. You can move forward, solve problems, or hunt for solutions and be calm at the same time. You don't need to engage stress with every problem that pollutes your life.

You can engage calm and still pound through to-do lists with ease and flow.

Bliss out with positive affirmations

Affirmations are positive statements that affirm outcomes you seek. They are a powerful feel-good habit to support you. This is the practice of positive thinking. Bliss out on good feelings with the help of perpetual affirmations that help activate this high vibration inside you.

Affirmations need to be specific to you, based on what you want to accomplish and how you want to feel. When you create them, make them specific and lively. Affirm what you want, not what you don't want. Some examples:

- I am joyful, and I am appreciative for a loving, accepting life partner.

- I am happy and grateful I am living in my beautiful home on the beach.

- I am celebrating how fit and healthy I am.

  Notice the key elements:

- I am (not I will) is affirmative and present tense.

- The statements include positive emotion (embody the way you want to feel).

- They are specific.

- They are active.

- They are short.

- They focus on a want (not on something unwanted).

You wouldn't say, "I'm so glad I'm moving out of that dumpy apartment." This affirmation is talking about what you don't want (the old apartment). The subconscious mind isn't good with nuances. You have to speak to it affirmatively about a desired outcome. Instead you might say, "I'm so excited to move to a beautiful new apartment." Don't say, "I am relieved I'm not a lousy cook." (All the subconscious hears is that you are a bad cook.) Instead, say, "I'm so glad I can cook these healthy, delicious meals with ease."

It's simply the good feelings you're after. When possible, let go of all hustle toward your goal and just bliss out on those good vibes.

Uplifting feelings keep you primed for success. From time to time, you will find old patterns like fear and anger clinging to you, trying to take over. You will sniff out the sinking feelings as they drag you further into a downward spiral. Generate emotions like compassion, gratitude, and joy with affirmations. Elevate your climb forward into your life with positive energy. Stay in these good feelings as long as you can.

For inspiration, you will find sets of affirmations sprinkled throughout this book. Use them to uplift you. Use them, along with other tools in this book, to embody positive feelings in the present moment. These affirmations may seem simple, and they are, because feeling good is simple. Stress is complicated, happiness isn't.

Affirmations are a fun, simple, and legal way to instantaneously feel good.

The more playfully we go about blissing out, the easier it is.

AFFIRMATIONS TO LOVE YOUR LIFE AS IT IS

I am exactly where I need to be.

I love my life.

Life gives me everything I want.

I grow smarter every day.

I look forward to every day.

My life improves every day.

My dreams are becoming a reality.

I trust the universe to bring me what I need.

I am confident and capable.

I have a positive outlook.

Everything is a learning experience.

I appreciate life.

It's okay when things don't go as planned.

· · · FEEL-GOOD HABITS · · ·

1 **Raise your vibration with affirmations.** These empowering mantras meaningfully affect your subconscious. State them in the present tense as if they are happening now. Declare the condition you desire to be true. You can more easily attract what you desire if you fully believe it's possible. Create a higher vibration to attract happiness.

I suggest you pick up two or three affirmations at a time. Bliss out on them several times a day for a few minutes at a time. Stay with them and repeat them until they cause a natural positive feeling every time you think of them. The more you return to these affirmations the more activated inside you they will become. To bliss out is to practice a higher vibration.

They will start to easily unravel positive feelings to propel your day forward. Use them often in the morning to give yourself a good energy boost and get out in front of your day with positive momentum.

Read your affirmations aloud or write them out in your journal, repetitively, every day. Repeat them in your head six to ten times in the morning and at night. Revel in the feelings of joy and success inside you. Imagine the affirmation being true, bliss out on how good it makes you feel. This technique is like digging around in your subconscious mind with a backhoe, removing doubt, but without heavy lifting—it happens easily, with just the power of your thoughts.

2   **Bliss out to get your direction right.** Whenever you have a problem, immediately focus on a solution. The longer you complain about the problem the worse you will feel. Instead, imagine moving toward what you want. For instance: A project you're working on is going sideways; people are disappointed. As soon as you can, imagine things working out. Visualize everything coming together and people feeling good about your work. This doesn't require anyone or anything to change. Just bliss out for at least seventeen seconds on the good feelings of opportunity and a successful project moving forward. Do this until those good feelings gain traction and flourish inside you.

Your launching point for solving problems is to feel good about your situation first. Once you feel better, the new focused clarity will reveal opportunities and attract solutions and support. The only limits you have are in your imagination.

3   **Notice your conditions.** Understanding the conditions you place on your good vibes is actually pretty simple. Below are a few examples. From these examples make a list of the ways you label conditions. It will help if you have fun with this activity and do not take yourself too seriously. The best way to lift conditions is to not focus on them.

You don't like your wrinkles.
The condition: You can't have wrinkles and be happy.

You don't like your extra ten pounds.
The condition: You can't carry this extra weight and be happy.

You haven't been given a raise in three years.
The condition: You need a raise to enjoy your job.

You're tired of cleaning up after your family.
The condition: You need everyone to pitch in for you to be happy.

The stalled economy is bringing you down.
The condition: You need economic conditions to improve to move forward.

Recognize that your conditions create a strong point of attraction and cause you to focus on what you don't want. They are holding you back. You will move forward when you release them and focus on happiness, prosperity, hope, or any good feeling you chose. To get your direction right, always focus on where you're headed, not on where you are.

4   **Lift the conditions that are holding up happiness.** On a sheet of paper, work through the following steps, focusing on an area of life where you struggle (relationships, work, health). Let's use finances as an example. Say you have a $40,000 debt weighing on you. Ask:

- What is the problem am I hustling to fix? *I have massive debt, and I need to get rid of it.*

- What is the condition I am placing on success? *I need to be debt-free to be successful. Because I currently have debt, I cannot be successful or happy.*

- What do I really want? *I want prosperity.*

Notice how the third question changes your direction? You release the condition of *no debt* by flipping your focus. You choose a good-feeling label that is already inside you (feelings of prosperity, success, easily receiving money). You avoid a label like *debt-free* so you don't focus on the debt. With enough repetition, you will be able to bliss out on feelings of success and prosperity. As you practice and sustain this vibration, it will easily flow.

This book will give you lots of habits to nourish feelings of success inside you. The visualizations and positive affirmations in the pages to come will get your success energy moving. Obviously, you are still going to pay down your debt, and your focused thought will move you forward and feel good.

Bliss out on feelings of prosperity and success, and they will flow into your life.

2

LIFT YOUR HUSTLE HANGOVER

KEEP MOVING FORWARD

A T A young age, a strong work ethic was drilled into me. My father was a workaholic, and I followed in his footsteps. I believed I had to hustle, work harder than others to earn my place in the world. I had to prove my worth, and effort was the only tool at my disposal.

Right out of college, I launched a marketing consulting company. It was immediately successful because I took a unique approach. I scanned the yellow pages for associations, called them up, and told them I would give their small-business members a speech for free. My talk was about a mistake commonly made by such companies: not having a proper marketing plan. At the end of the speech, I revealed I was available to write those plans. Many took the bait, hired me, and I snared plenty of clients right away.

But I had a problem. I didn't want to write marketing plans, and I didn't really have the skills to do it. Soon enough, some of those clients caught on to me and wanted their money back. I was getting desperate. I felt sick that I was disappointing people. Even when I surprised myself with success, I stumbled on doubt.

If I just work harder, I told myself, *I can fix this.* I hunkered down and toiled away at market plans that all my clients threw back at me in disappointment. Then I locked myself in my apartment for days, reworking the plans that had been met with disdain. Finally, I needed to come up for air.

I had a hustle hangover. So, I took a break from my toxic work ethic and headed to the bar. That night, I ran into my former, still youngish, marketing professor. He wanted to sleep with me, and I wanted to hire him to write marketing plans for my clients.

That night, we both got what we wanted. I put him on the payroll and ran around giving speeches for any small-business group that would listen. He worked on the plans, and I escaped overbearing fear and doubt, for the moment.

One day I came across a yellow pages listing for an association of professional speakers. I thought it was talking about sound systems, which I found incredibly boring. I called the number and gave the man on the line my spiel to speak to his members. He laughed and advised me that *they* were professional speakers. I thought, *You think because you put the word* professional *in front, you are more important?* They badly needed marketing advice.

He invited me to come to a meeting for free. Hey, that was my racket! It was also exactly what I was willing to pay, so I agreed. I showed up at the Saturday-morning meeting with a raging hangover, still thinking we were there to talk about the ins and outs of sound systems. I stumbled in late, and the first presentation had already started. I couldn't find a seat, so I stood at the back.

This moment, the man speaking at the front of the room, changed my life.

I wasn't sure what he was trying to do to us, but he wasn't selling sound systems.

The short bow-tie-wearing fellow holding the microphone altered my entire direction. His words and energy awakened something inside me. It was weird and dangerously exciting. No one had ever told me that I had potential or that taking on

There is one glaring problem with hard work: **it has to be hard for it to work.**

a perspective of hope and possibility could change my life. In forty-five minutes, my self-loathing, toxic work ethic, and doubt were erased and replaced with hope and inspiration.

The man with the microphone was superbly spoken and charismatic. He made me laugh, he made me cry. He was a *motivational* speaker. I hadn't known that people like this existed. But I knew I wanted to be one.

The pure, powerful potential I felt in the room that morning was not subtle. It initiated immediate momentum. The man's inspiring words hit me just the right way to transform a challenging career into a fun adventure. I fired my clients, dumped my marketing professor, joined the professional speakers association, and started anew.

Since then, I've often felt unstoppable in my career. In other areas of my life, like relationships, financial investments, and health, I have often felt stuck. But in my career, most of the time, I have an inner knowing that I can accomplish whatever I set out for, and that I don't have to hustle more than others to achieve it. I replaced my tough work ethic with the belief that as long as I am inspired, I can inspire.

Hustling for what?

Does hard work make you happy? Anything difficult usually doesn't make me happy.

Because I had a hard-work ethic drilled into me as a child, sometimes I work so hard that I have to come up for air. My head feels dense, my thoughts fuzzy. I feel worn out. I start fantasizing about fear. I feel like I have a hangover.

The word *hangover* originates in the early nineteenth century as an expression describing unfinished business from meetings. Its original use related to unfinished work hanging from one day over to the next.[4]

This is what hard work feels like—it's always unfinished, never done. It keeps hanging over your head, even when you're not working, a constant reminder of duty and struggle.

I don't think many people want to sign up for work that's going to be hard. But we've all been told we have to work hard to get ahead. It is so confusing—no wonder people keep tainting morale, passion, and all these great positive feelings with work ethic.

And then we get stifled by negative thoughts, fear, worry, and doubt that pinch off our momentum. It handcuffs progress and dashes hopes. We may be too focused on hard effort instead of progress and possibilities, putting our hustle ahead of happiness and feelings of success.

For instance, your job was meant to be an opportunity to make money and learn stuff. If you feel stuck in your job, it's a bummer because you're not moving forward like you wanted. You didn't get the promotion, and the job doesn't allow you to be as productive as you had hoped it would. That's disappointing. So, maybe you tag your work ethic and ramp up your hustle to prove yourself.

But just remember you don't have to work for happiness, you already have it. Feelings of success are inside you too. They don't require your effort. Joy and success are an internal thought and feeling vibration and not dependent on your workload. Joy is not a goal, it's a feeling. If you remove the condition of ideal workloads, you see the joy and potential right there inside you.

Moving toward potential

Although I've always believed I chose a fun, successful career, I have felt stuck in other areas of my life, like in financial situations and relationships. I know how draining that is. It's hard to work at it and not see progress.

If you feel stuck, it is probably because you are. The circumstances of your life may not appeal to you, and that draining feeling holds you back. When you don't get what you want, disappointment can reach inside you and limit your joy. But you need the momentum of positive emotions to move forward.

Take for example my many ambitious, career-oriented friends who decide they want to find a spouse. They go after this goal with diligent focus. I see them constantly irritated, frustrated, and stuck in the process. Here's why... They think, *If I want a spouse, I just go and get one.* But it's not that easy, right? He has to be tall, funny, charming, smart—and these prospects are already taken.

But what they really desire is love. and now they've placed all these conditions on it. Unless love presents itself as tall, funny, rich, and charming, they won't even see it. Maybe, like my friends, you hustle around dating websites and crowded bars searching for the perfect spouse. But love has been there all along, inside. If you take that love and throw it all over your life, an equal amount of love will find you.

I'm suggesting you routinely focus on feelings of appreciation for your cat, your father, or the woman at the post office that always makes you smile. Instead of focusing on a lack of affection in your life, focus on the love you desire. Always give your attention to what you *want*, not what you don't want.

Let your emotions guide you. Whenever you feel stifled in your path toward love, you'll feel bad. This is your cue to lift whatever conditions you placed on love (tall, handsome, funny, rich), let go of the hustle, and bliss out in happiness and love instead. Focus on the deficiencies of the prospects in front of you, and you'll always uncover more deficiencies. Focus on the love inside you, and it will grow, expand, and flourish. Love, in turn, will find you.

Love may not look tall, fit, and sexy. It might even be chubby and bald, but if it's real it will be powerful and extraordinary.

True, unbound love will always propel you forward and you'll never feel stuck. If you do feel stuck, conditions you place on love are stalling you. They are creating doubt and holding you back.

You chose your job, your house, your spouse (or anything at all) because you saw its potential. Everything you have chosen landed in your lap because you saw it as an opportunity to improve your life. You went to school to build a better future, you tried online dating to find a great spouse, you became a lawyer to impress your mother, you bought your car because you need it to get to work. Every day, you make multiple decisions with the primary goal of improving your life and moving forward.

This drive within you to move forward is a magical thing. It speaks to an intense desire to re-create, innovate, and improve your life. It gives you purpose, meaning, and hope.

In your life you want to blaze ahead, and you should. If you can stop tripping up this positive momentum with fear and doubt, you will.

Don't hustle—believe!

Anytime you feel stuck you will be tempted to hustle around controlling the problem, people involved, and outcomes. Instead, skip a beat and believe! Unleash this powerful force into your life. Here's an example: Kerri used to work for me. When I first hired her she was productive and enthusiastic. Eventually, her good attitude started to wane. She called in sick a lot and did not meet expectations. I had to let her go, but not before I spent endless hours fretting over her attitude and performance.

My worrisome thoughts weren't helping. They built a palpable resentment between us. I kept thinking, *Why can't she just do what I say? Her behavior is a problem. If only she'd listen, we'd be okay.* No wonder the relationship didn't work—controlling other people never does. Rather than trying to direct

The energy
of success and
prosperity
is in you.

her actions, I could have believed in her strengths and inspired her with purpose and passion. This energy would have moved us both forward. Instead our relationship fell apart.

One of the best lessons I continue to learn is that we can't control people.

I've seen many well-intentioned, determined people try, and all it usually does is make for a good first marriage. And a second or third marriage, for the slow learners.

Eventually, we clue in that people can't be controlled, and every effort to do so just takes us further from what we want. It irritates and confuses.

Controlling people means you need them to act in a prescribed way for you to be happy or successful. This snares your powerful desire, belief, and potential in a net of attachment to circumstances and people. The energy dynamic is fear, worry, or lack. It holds you back.

Belief

Behind every goal is a desire, a craving for progress. This powerful, optimistic force can build momentum inside you and attract success. Instead of pushing people or circumstances around, you line up with your desire and belief in success.

You inspire others with your enthusiasm and belief rather than controlling and limiting them.

The energy around hustle and effort is often attached to fear, lack, and doubt and propels you to control outcomes, while belief is boundless and powered by feelings of success.

Every thought and resulting feeling you have is practicing an energy vibration that either moves you forward or holds you back.

Bliss out on belief in your abilities, and you will have no reason to hustle.

Feeling good moves you forward

Can you remember back to when you chose your current job or your spouse? Can you remember how they made you feel? Probably pretty good because that's why you chose them. If, at the time, you thought that dating your future spouse was a waste of time or that you were better than the job offer in front of you, you would not be where you are today.

You only move forward in life when you feel good. Remembering that is so important. It's why you need to put good feelings ahead of the hustle toward goals.

Problems arise because every time we expect external circumstances to make us happy, they don't.

Consider that in any area of your life you feel bad about (a person you have conflict with, a stalled work project, your child's poor math scores), the bad feelings contribute to your disgruntled situation. When you invest negative thoughts and feelings into those scenarios, they limit you. The negative emotions build up a magnetic charge that lures you back to those thoughts. Pretty soon you are holding negative circumstances in your life through your attention to them.

What you really want is to lift these conditions and climb into life. With positive emotions you can move toward your children, your spouse, your job, and everything in your life rather than away from it all.

Take Khalil, for example. Khalil is a project manager working on a new building downtown. Recently, his permits were pulled and that has slowed down his whole team. Instead of making progress on their vision, they are contending with mounds of paperwork and a legal battle.

At first, Khalil and his team got mad because the circumstances changed. Now they are stalled. His team could spend years fighting the government, their investors, and one another until those permits are approved. Embroiled in the fight is a lot of negativity and backward momentum. Every time they have to file a lawsuit or prove their design, they feel worried and depleted.

But all this team wants is to move forward on this amazing project and to feel good about their contribution. The pulled permit is stalling and frustrating them. But what if they changed their momentum by shifting their thoughts and feelings about the project, the permit, the lawyers, and the government? What if they clung to the original hope and possibility they felt about the project? They would start to move forward. What if they saw the government not as a villain stalling them but as a partner helping them? That's also moving forward. If they thought and felt good about the design changes being asked of them, their potential to improve the project would be obvious to them too.

If this team could feel really good about this project despite circumstances and spread that enthusiasm to the government and their investors, their project would gain traction. If Khalil and his team were to bliss out on feelings of passion, purpose, and pride for their project, the vibrant magnetic energy would make them unstoppable.

Seeing the problems hurled in front of us as potential will move us in the right direction. This often takes steady belief, hope, enthusiasm, and positivity, but when our hope and enthusiasm is stronger than our fear and doubt, we always win.

Appreciate—don't tolerate

Years ago I was strung out and exhausted with a heavy travel schedule. I felt so depleted that I was disinclined to appreciate life. Good things were happening around me every day, and I completely tuned them out.

Just thinking about expressing gratitude for my life felt like a chore. I shrugged it off and rationalized that clinging to gratitude is something only desolate people do to get by. *I'm too busy and important to worry about cherishing life.*

If your life is geared to hustling around after goals all the time, it's a tough way to live. Even gratitude becomes an obligation. You feel indebted to appreciation instead of actually feeling it. You tolerate life instead of living it. But you don't have to prove to anyone else that you appreciate your life. You just have to convince yourself.

There is so much more joy on the other side of stress, and all we have to do is give our attention to it. If you can keep up with appreciation for the life you have, you pave the way for so much more to come.

You don't need to hustle around Neiman Marcus seeking approval from others or collecting more stuff, appreciation is a feeling inside you that will blossom anytime you pay attention. It will increasingly feel good to you every time you lollygag in gratitude. Now you're enjoying the journey. Bliss out on appreciation for your life—with these good vibes flowing, success is a sure thing.

Ambition—the powerful drive that wants more

Ambition. It's that aching desire that wants more. It's a powerful invisible force, and it's not contained in your big toe or your elbow. Your drive and ambition show up everywhere you look. Goals are alluring because you can see them being accomplished, you can even benchmark and brag about them to your grandmother.

But where is your ambition? It seems invisible, but it's not. Ambition is in your steely gaze, your tight grip on the future. Your refusal to give up. Your hankering to right wrongs. Pieces of ambition are deeply embedded in your fear of letting people down. Ambition pounces on you when you fall short of your goals. When you hide in the bathroom stall because you fear your boss's rejection, ambition scolds you too.

It surrounds you. Your ambition is in your child's frustration when she doesn't ace her math quiz and places unforgiving demands on herself. Your ambition is in your spouse's flicker of disappointment when work steals your time from your family. Ambition scolds you when the economy crumbles. It's proudly displayed in your trophy case in the family living room. It's in the green smoothie you guzzle down before work. It's affirmed by your day planner and properly contained in your neatly organized files at work.

Ambition has given you so much, but did you have to struggle so hard to get it? What if you let go of the worry, doubt, and fear and just went for what you wanted?

The energy of success and prosperity is in you, too, but it doesn't get any stage time in a goal-oriented environment. You hustle toward your goals, expecting to see outcomes. Your invisible uplifting thoughts and emotional momentum, however, are what bring results. You need to believe in success first; believe in the good feelings, and the success will follow. Turn your focus toward and nourish the powerful, optimistic force inside you to propel you in the direction of your dreams.

Instead of righting wrong, doubting yourself, and fearing failure, let your positive belief and energy propel you and others forward.

Ambition causes you to hustle, but you can get what you want without the struggle—just let passion guide you.

Who, me? Ambitious?

Ambitious people are often goal-setters. Not necessarily goals with specific progress and deadlines pinned to them, although those are included. Often ambition is just an inner drive to improve. If you're not big on setting goals, don't for a second think that excludes you from the ambitious crew.

Ambition simply means you want to move forward. This is what everyone wants. Just because you're not a hustler doesn't mean you want your efforts to be fruitless. We usually see ambitious people as determined, sometimes obsessed, high achievers. Yet, I've met many ambitious stay-at-home parents, dog walkers, and hairdressers. I've met clerks working at Walmart who ooze ambition.

Don't exclude yourself from ambition if your life doesn't look like images of lawyers on Netflix. Ambition is inside you, too. If you attach your ambition to extraneous conditions, you will discover where stress resides. Because ambition is fickle. It makes you feel bad and pulls you from your possibilities. It lowers your vibration.

The word *ambition* means a strong desire to achieve something. This usually requires determination and hard work. It's a motivation and it wants a resolution. It wants you to conquer a goal, so you call on your hustle and work ethic to fuel the quest.

But while ambition sometimes requires hard work and hustle, it doesn't have to. Instead of focusing on results and effort, you can choose potential. Bliss out on the feeling of success, and let those good vibes propel you to it. Before you take any action, just determine your direction. Are you focused on good feelings and inspiration to move you forward, or are you focused on problems, stress, and conflict?

If you're broke, you don't have to panic and start renting your backyard out to campers. Consider blissing out on feelings of prosperity instead.

Consider this: when you achieve a goal, it shows up in your life. If your goal is to make money, you will see more money in your bank account. And if you don't see that money? You'll aggravate the hustle and place conditions on success. In this

It doesn't matter what you do, **it matters how you feel about what you do.**

case, more cash. Now, suddenly, you need money to be successful, and you don't have it. You don't meet your own condition.
You put effort and the hustle ahead of the happiness and prosperity that allows success to flow.

You're headed toward a hustle hangover. Just like with any
addiction, you need to know when to quit.

Does this mean quit your job or stop trying? No, it just means
change your direction. You need to be under the influence of
happiness and success, not hustle, lack of money, and hard work.

To do this, pay attention to how you feel, good or bad, so you
know if you are heading in the direction of your goals. When
you flip your attention and live your goals from the inside out,
you nurture the thoughts and beliefs first. Success is an energy
inside you. It's been there all along. So, tap into feelings of happiness and prosperity, and then see what happens.

Anytime you move your focus off your internal positive
good feelings about your goal and onto the circumstances surrounding achieving it, you may feel depleted. If so, you need to
smother those circumstances with positive energy. Bliss out on
those buoyant feelings any chance you can. The only reason a
problem looks like a problem is because of the labels and constraints you place on your passion. Lift those labels. Focus on
the joy of the journey, not the destination.

The more I believe in passion, the more I see that problems
aren't problems, they are just information guiding me to remove
conditions. They are nudging me toward potential.

Potential is undefined. It isn't created yet. It's also unlimited, so you can't place a target on it. Success and prosperity are
feelings and energy inside you. When you box them into goals,
hustle, effort, and timelines, you stifle their flow.

If you believe in the feeling of success and let it loose inside
you, the feeling will always nudge you toward its potential real-
ization. You still go for your goals, and you feel good while you
do it.

Throughout this book, I am introducing you to positive affirmations and visualizations as some of the most powerful habits to nurture positive momentum. The real goal is always to put the good feeling inside you *now* and let it flourish.

Believe in this powerful invisible force to move you in the right direction.

AFFIRMATIONS FOR WORK

I work at a job I enjoy.
I am respected by my colleagues.
I learn every day.
I have a wonderful relationships with members of my team.
My boss appreciates me.
I attract praise.
I praise others.
I bring unique skills to my job.
My workplace cares about me.
My skills are in demand.
I am all I can be.
I honor my purpose and inspire others.
I am focused and persistent.
I line up my emotions with my decisions.
I have renewed confidence every day.
I improve every day.

Hey, hustler, does work have to be hard?

Have you ever been driving to work secretly hoping your workplace blew up? Just so you wouldn't have to go? I have.

Work translates to trading our time and effort for money. Most of the time it's assumed we don't want to do it—otherwise, they wouldn't have to pay us. Work is usually a thorn in our side, we have to sacrifice to get the job done.

Money is just a piece of paper designed so we wouldn't have to kill each other for food. Yet, it's very powerful. It shapes our actions and decisions. It can also bend our attitude about work so we perceive it as a hassle. Whenever someone utters the word *work*, it has an air of challenge, burden, stress, and responsibility around it. They pay us money, and we labor to complete the tasks assigned.

Why would I want to spend over half my life doing something painstaking and potentially oppressive? Maybe choosing a career as a stripper wouldn't be as bad as a torturous, boring career. Ever since we were young, we were told the proper thing to do is to grow up and get a job. I want to be useful; however, I don't enjoy tribulations that make me miserable. But this is the way we describe work. If I could opt out of work, I would. It sounds dreadful.

It's a good idea to understand your motives around your work. Think about your job: If you weren't being paid, would you still do it?

This isn't an argument for marrying rich, instead, it's an invitation to rethink the way you position work in your mind. What if we lifted the obligation and hard effort assumed by your ambitious work ethic?

The moment we paint anything as *hard* it becomes more difficult to do. Just because people pay us, doesn't mean working needs to be a burden. As you dart around ticking off items on your to-do list, is it your sense of obligation that pesters you to complete things? Most of the time it is. The trouble with this is your ambition is guaranteed by stress, placing constraints on happiness. Stress is driving you to complete your tasks. The whole routine is held together by chasing problems like cavemen chasing their next meal. It's deficiency and problems that drive our ambition, not inspiration or purpose. The ambition for more happiness is inside you, it's unlimited. By pinning it down, you're limiting it. You're better than that.

Also, the solutions you chase around outside yourself are hinged on circumstances and other people's approval. The endless supply of hope and optimism inside you is a force that can well up and give you boundless energy. It will respond to an invitation to support you. You can do the same or more work, but without the hassle of stress nagging you.

1 **Bliss out on your to-do list.** It doesn't matter what you do, it matters how you feel about what you do. Review your to-do list. How does it make you feel? Excited or drained? Notice if you chase after problems to quell doubt. Divorce yourself from your tough work ethic for a moment and think about the possibility and potential. Bring it into the now. Raise your vibration about your to-do list. Bliss out on good feelings about it for seventeen seconds to activate the good vibes. Sit and marinate in these good feelings for a while. I suggest you do this first thing in the morning to propel good energy out in front of your day.

For instance, an item on my to-do list is to categorize my receipts for my accountant. I'd rather watch paint dry. But when I connected my receipts to my overall mission of inspiring people, I could see it as an essential part of possibilities and growth. When I itemize receipts, I bring the feeling of prosperity and flow into me. I use the money I earn from my work to pay for the items I need. Overall, this cycle fuels the economy. It fuels my business. It's creating possibility, not draining me and my future.

Actively connect possibilities with activities that otherwise bring you down. Imagine doing these things with a sense of fun, ease, and efficiency.

2 **Break the habit of telling it like it is.** Instead, tell it like you want it to be. Move the direction of your thoughts toward what you want several times a day. For instance, when it

rains, look forward to a sunny day. Think about how great it feels to bask in the sun. Bliss out on thoughts of the sunlight burning through the clouds. Will this change the weather? No. But you will feel good and move your day forward.

3 **Boost joy in your job.** Would you still work if they didn't pay you? Is there any part of your work that you would still do? Through this inquiry, you can discover the parts of your job you enjoy and work on feeling gratitude for them. A gratefulness routine involves recognizing and focusing on the positive aspects of your work a few times in your day—try doing this over the next week. Every day, enjoy making a list of what you appreciate about your work. I like to write mine down to reinforce it. Use repetition and write the same things over and over again. While you write about the things you enjoy in your job, bliss out on the good feelings this brings.

4 **Describe your intentions.** It helps to recognize your intentions before you let ambition loose on your goals. Take any activity you completed in your day and ask yourself where your focus was. Were you focused on problems or solutions? Let's say you have a conflict with a contractor. In your interaction was your goal to fix them (or the situation), to teach them a lesson, or was it to work with harmony and purpose? What if, instead, your intention was to strengthen your relationship and better understand hiccups in your workflow? Or your intention could be to see opportunities. Was your intention driven by fear, conflict, or doubt, or was it driven by joy and opportunity? You can easily see how results could differ based on your intention. Now take that same activity

and flip your focus to look forward at opportunities, success, and potential.

5   **Line up with your decisions.** When you choose a spouse, a job, a new laundry detergent, or anything at all—line up with that decision. This means believe in it and wipe away any doubt or worry. Once you choose someone or something, go along with your decision and turn your back on any niggling doubts. Just believe. Routinely reinforce to yourself all positive aspects of your decision.

3

NAME YOUR BLISS

INFUSE YOUR LIFE WITH POSITIVE LABELS

DON'T BELONG in Nordstrom—I'd never pay a thousand bucks for a T-shirt. Besides, I couldn't even get in the building, the one time I tried. I stood outside Nordstrom pushing forcefully on the door, unable to budge it.

Until I heard a kind voice behind me say, "Pull the door toward you, dear." I pulled lightly, and the door flew open. I entered the world of glamor. I still couldn't afford anything, but it was nice to be inside.

Most of my life, I've been a pusher. So are the majority of people. We push ourselves out of bed in the morning, push our kids to get ready for school. We push papers around at work. People push priorities on us, that we push ourselves to complete. We push open doors of opportunity. We push back deadlines and push customers to buy. We undercut our prices and push our competitors out of the market. Inside any push is usually some sort of conflict that you need to resolve.

All day, we push. We label our life as hard, and we have to push it away. It's exhausting. I'm not sure what we're pushing for, but I think it has to do with staking a claim on our future. Until someone comes along and teaches you to pull, and with so much less effort, doors open for you.

Anytime we push things around, we are focused on our problems, creating a strong resistance. We just need the gentle reminder to focus on what we want instead of what we don't. The best way to enjoy the journey is to move from resisting life (labeling it as bad and pushing it away) to pulling it in and allowing and appreciating it. From here we start to see potential.

It all starts with how you label people and circumstances in your life. To really experience life, you appreciate and feel good about it without the label.

I used to be really curious about this flower that sprouts up between the cracks in the sidewalk. One day a friend of mine told me it's called bitter cress, and it's a common weed. Now that I had a label for this plant, I was much less curious. Instead of pondering its beauty, I simply shrugged it off and carried on with my day. I enjoyed that flower much more before it had a label.

Many of the labels we put on things limit our expansive perspective and enjoyment. In life, new faces and places can offer the same conclusions or they can reach toward bliss and potential.

What's most limiting is when we haplessly apply those labels on ourselves and others.

Labels that limit

I used to have a group of new age friends. We took workshops on self-development together. One course taught us to call each other out on our "stuff." We would regularly call each other by labels that defined our inadequacies. Brenda was *cheap*. Sarah was *always tired*. Michael was *perpetually late*. Sal was a *people pleaser*. Monique was a *constant worrier*. And I was *too hardworking*.

We thought that, because we were so personally evolved, we could handle the feedback. In reality, because our close circle of friends kept reminding us of our deficiencies, we became more and more like our labels. Brenda's cheapness meant she never had any money. Sarah was too exhausted to do anything. We were always waiting on Michael. Sal kept rearranging his life to get our approval. Monique worried about everyone, and I was just too busy working.

Anytime you label something, it gives your brain direction, and gathers more of your attention. You attract more thoughts like it. For example, a friend recently bought a Tesla. It's a beautiful car and good for the environment. Before, I didn't know these cars existed—they never came across my radar—but now everywhere I go, I see them on the road.

This is the power of your point of attraction. Every thought you have attracts more thoughts just like it to you. You'll start noticing and appreciating more of it in your life. My friend also routinely calls herself a *poor listener*. This label works just like the Tesla. She keeps gathering evidence that suggests she has inferior listening skills. She is a bad listener because she chose that label; she gives purpose to her weakness, not her strengths.

A negative label limits you because it gets your attention more often than opportunity, joy, appreciation, or love.

Unsurprisingly, that group of friends I mentioned dissolved. I still remain addicted to personal-development advice, though, because I have a sense there is more to life than what we're living.

The trouble with the term *self-help* is that it implies you need help. Your deficiencies become your focus. There is nothing wrong with you at all; you don't necessarily need what the label suggests you do.

If you seek out your inner strength, however, you may just bliss out in what you discover.

You never have to work for good feelings—**they are inside you right now.**

Labeling your strengths is a feel-good habit

Recently, at the post office, I walked to the other end of the counter to get a pen but was distracted by a text message. I got back to my parcel and said, "Oh, I forgot the pen." Someone in line pointed out, "No, you remembered it."

Did I forget or remember? The answer depends on where I put my attention: on my weakness or my strength. I can naturally laser in on poor memory (weakness) and attract more fear and doubt. Or, I can recognize that to notice what I forgot I have to remember (strength).

Always focus on your strengths rather than your weaknesses.

Label your strengths. Since we love to put labels on ourselves and others, why not choose embellishments like *optimistic, smart, fun, kind*, and *successful*? These are positive labels. You can tell by their glorious forward-feeling momentum, they move us toward our potential and make us feel good.

A reliable feel-good habit is to label your life positively. Go ahead. Why not choose a positive label for yourself right now? How do you know it's the right label for you? It makes you feel good.

Call yourself *fun, kind, full of potential, loving, supportive, successful, engaged, calm, prosperous, proud, optimistic, happy, confident, appreciative*, and so on. As long as the label makes you feel good, you're on the right track.

A feeling, not a goal

A label should be bestowed on you because it's a feeling not a goal. You may be tempted to call yourself *charming*, but this is more like a quality you have to earn than a feeling. You never have to work for good feelings, they are inside you. Right now. Thus instead of saying you are *funny*, which entails the pressure to perform for others by telling jokes and making people laugh (a goal), label yourself as *fun*, which is a feeling inside you. You don't have to work for fun, you just have to be open to experience it. Go on! Feel it. Bliss out on a feeling of fun for a while.

The joy of an experience comes in your good feelings. When your positive label causes you to feel good, you expand toward life instead of limiting your experience by labeling and judging it. All that matters is that the label makes you feel good. For instance, *success* is a feeling, but it's also a goal. You're going to focus on the feeling. Even if you haven't reached your tangible goal of success, you can still *feel* successful. And you should because it will get you where you want to go.

Always focus on the good feeling a label gives you and less on any action or goal it may compel you to achieve. For instance, you could label yourself a *kind mom*, this would be so rewarding. You will be tempted to hustle around doing kind things for your kids. But what if you concentrated on the thoughts and feelings versus the doing? What if you thought often about being a loving parent, about understanding and appreciating your kids? How would that make you feel inside? Notice and feel good about acts of kindness around you. Think kind thoughts about your kids, their teachers and other parents. Point out when your kids are kind to each other and recognize how good it makes everyone feel. You're not trying to manipulate others (or yourself) to be kind; but all the same, you are reminiscing about how great kindness feels. Instead of forcing kindness you bliss out on feelings of kindness that transform your relationships.

Your good feelings help you appreciate your experiences and the real joy of the journey.

These labels are warm and life-changing things for you to feel, not goals for you to conquer. It will always be rewarding to bliss out on positive feelings. Nobody has to earn them, and there is *no hustle here.*

Positive labels will help you get out in front of your day and drive it forward with positive emotion. Before you take any action at all, you can set yourself up for a happy day by labeling it a *good day*.

If you labeled your day as *easy*, your work as *rewarding*, your relationships as *fun*, you could bliss out on these feelings for a while, and the positive momentum would move you forward.

The hard-work (hustle) label

The word *hustle* means to obtain by forceful action or persuasion. This is how most people work, through hustle and action.

I want to throw some compassion at you right now, because giving up the hard-work label is not always easy. Throughout our lives, people have told us hard work is a good thing. And it is, if it means progress, which usually it does. But this label doesn't help us. It's the *hard* part that induces hustle. Labeling anything as a struggle means it will always be hard. You'll have to apply force to get what you want. Often, for you to win, others have to lose.

Let's lift this label because it's conditioning us to believe success only comes from struggle and outdoing others. Let's use words like *fun, purposeful,* and *rewarding* to describe work. Any project you are working on, infuse it with a positive label—this will help you move forward and feel good.

In fact, you might like to ditch the label *work*. The only reason it's called work is because people pay us. That part is usually a given, so why not call it something else? Work for meaning rather than money. This way your intention is always focused on adding meaning to others instead of gaining money for yourself. While collecting money stops at you, meaning is a forward-moving label that keeps expanding.

Positive labels

The question I get asked the most about public speaking is, "Do you ever get nervous?" I always give the same response. Fear and excitement are similar feelings; they are both jumpy. So I just label my nerves as *excitement* and public speaking as *fun*. All I know is that every time I give a speech, I am bursting with excitement and the time just flies by. Public speaking is fun, rewarding, and exciting, all because of this label. If I ever got into the routine of saying, "I hate public speaking," or, "I get nervous when I speak," I would have never chosen (or survived) this career.

What positive labels do you want to infuse into your life?

You can label your positive attributes (good memory, vibrant health, happiness) and you can label important activities or aspects of your life favorably. For instance, your work is *fun*, or serving your customers is *rewarding*. Look for anything you are passionate about in your job and label it positively so you can more easily line up with it instead of resisting it.

While you are at it, infuse a positive label on some of your most important relationships. For instance, your spouse is *supportive*, your son is *smart* and *kind*, your neighbor is *appreciative*.

Positive labels help you move forward in your life because they focus on what you want in the future, and they make you feel good in the present. When you think your spouse is *loving* and *supportive*, this emotion will pull you toward him. You will spend more time with him and feel more positive, loving emotion about him. This forward momentum is climbing into your life because your spouse is in your life.

If you label that same spouse as *selfish* and *narcissistic*, you will find yourself resisting and moving away from him. You will argue more often, and you will do things to escape his presence. You will descend into these negative thoughts and emotions and away from this part of your life that involves him. Negative thoughts and emotions will always cause you to resist things in your life.

If you label your job as *meaningful* and *rewarding,* your thoughts and energy will build positive momentum toward a more meaningful and rewarding job. If you label your job as *annoying* and *frustrating,* your thoughts and feelings toward it will start pushing you away from it. You'll call in sick and find reasons not to be there. The work will seem more and more uncomfortable as you continue to dread it.

Notice how your thoughts and feelings are what create your momentum and direction. It's tantalizing to think it's your spouse or your job conditions at the root of your misery, but it's not. It's you. Your labels work just like pushing on the gas or the brakes of your car. Positive labels propel you forward in life, and negative labels stall you.

Labels give direction

You can always get your direction right by remembering a label is a feeling, not a doing. For instance, when you give someone a positive label, they never have to do anything to earn it. You give it generously. You feel good about them, because of the label, even when they haven't done anything to earn your good feelings. Those feelings are inside you—the reward is within. You now have your direction right.

I once had a tenant who constantly complained. I thought of her as *that difficult tenant.* I learned to avoid her requests. This really angered her, and I always felt annoyed. We had a definite negative momentum built up between us. Every time an email from her hit my inbox, I felt irritated. I didn't even have to read it; I knew it would contain a conflict.

I decided to let compassion take over, to label her as a *kind business partner*. Sometimes she called me up and started swearing at me; she was anything but kind. But I let the kindness label prevail. I pulled in her request and listened. I smothered my resistance and irritation with love. I saturated my feelings for her with acceptance and kindness.

She would complain about many things, but once I stopped pushing her away I learned she was struggling. She had been living with a cancer diagnosis for more than a year and was fighting for her life. I felt compassion and empathy. The negative thoughts and feelings I had for her were completely erased. I found out that underneath all the complaints, she was kind and doing the best she could.

I also came to see that everything she complained about was legit. If I were in her shoes, I'd be annoyed too. I could have done the repairs she was asking for much sooner, and none of the negativity we both struggled with would have existed. My negative feelings had stalled me and her.

People around you don't need a terminal diagnosis for you to feel compassion for them. That compassion is inside you and accessible at any time. And if you can learn to accept whatever life throws at you instead of resisting and glaring at its deficiencies, you will open up to potential.

Reaching outside for answers to what's wrong inside, you will always create turmoil. As soon as you label anything in life as bad, it will hold you back. The moment you decide to label something as positive, you start focusing on what you want. You start to move forward.

Always dial up your emotions because good feelings mean progress and potential. Keep your thoughts and feelings lined up with joy, appreciation, or love.

Most of the time we focus on external stimuli to bring us joy. That focus causes us to create conditions that limit joy. It sounds a lot like this: "If I get a new car, I'll be happy... When my spouse changes, I'll be happy... When I have more followers on Instagram, I'll be happy..."

Believe in your inner joy. Nourish it and don't let the world outside you irritate and limit it. The truth is, you can get a new car, a spouse you adore, and loads of Instagram followers, and these are byproducts of good labels and feelings.

Place a positive label on anything that stalls you in your job and start imagining it moving forward. Just aim to feel a little bit better about it, and eventually you'll feel good about it again.

For instance, that *difficult colleague* who keeps slowing down your progress with his rants? You need to lift that label. Choose anything positive that feels good. Does his eye for detail guide you to produce the best results? Perhaps he is someone who means well, and you can learn a lot from each other. Feel into labels that fit him. Is he perceptive, intelligent, or guiding you toward opportunities to expand your perspective? Make small jumps forward in good feelings, not huge leaps.

If your work is draining you, label your core work activities *easy* and *fulfilling*. Look at challenging tasks as *opportunities* and *potential*. Enjoy the labels and don't take yourself too seriously. This is not about analyzing results, it's about blissing out on good feelings.

It's also not wishful thinking. Many of these positive aspects are already true, but your doubt and negative label don't allow you to see this. Parts of your job flow easily and are actually fun. If you want to invite more of this positive flow and feeling (which you do), you have to focus more on these good-feeling aspects of your job.

Also, never go into a situation labeling it as *hard*. Because, guess what? It will be. If you label it as difficult, negative momentum will build. Instead think about all situations as *fun*, *easy*, and *loaded with opportunities*.

Here are more examples of changing the direction of a label from negative to positive:

GO FROM	TO
This is difficult.	Here's an opportunity to grow.
Things haven't improved.	Things are starting to look up.
It's too bad.	Here's what's good about it.
I'm worried about you.	Your strengths will get you through anything.
I'm concerned about . . .	I'm optimistic about . . .
It's scary.	I see potential.
You need to be more . . .	I appreciate you because . . .
I hate it when . . .	Isn't it great how . . .
If only . . .	I'm so glad that . . .

A positive label works if it makes you feel good. Also, notice the direction: negative labels are about the past and positive labels help propel you (and others) into the future.

As an ambitious person, you are used to commanding your life, so stress is a chief motivator. It calls on you to hustle hard. It holds the reins and pulls you this way and that to get things done. You need to change the narrative and invite in compassion, appreciation, and happiness. Stop pushing everything around and open up to happiness, love, and flow. It's actually simple: just lift your labels.

Believe in your inner joy.

Nourish it and don't let the world outside you irritate and limit it.

But I hate it when . . .

When you decide to feel bad about anything, just know it's a condition you label and place on your own happiness. Whenever you say something like "I hate it when . . .," you are placing a condition on your joy.

For instance, you love your spouse but hate it when they cut you off mid sentence. You've placed a conditional label on your love: you love them as long as they listen. You have stalled and limited your relationship. That makes you feel bad.

You like your commute but hate it when an accident slows traffic and makes you late for work. You enjoy driving as long as all your conditions are met. People need to drive safely, traffic needs to keep moving, and stupid drivers pretty much need to stay home. Then you are happy. But when you label every driver on the road as kind, helpful, and doing the best they can, your drive to work is a delight. You feel good as you witness all the good deeds unfolding around you.

This expansive perspective maintains curiosity and a willingness to grow.

Acceptance helps you relieve unforgiving conditions and ditch the labels by surrounding them with the benefit of the doubt. When things don't go the way you want, bring that in and look at it not as a problem but as potential. Appreciate the perspective it gives you.

AFFIRMATIONS TO INVITE CALM

I move through life with calm serenity.
I handle stress with ease.
I surround all stress with love.
My colleagues are so kind.
Everybody means well.
I release all doubt.
I feel alert and focused.
I am in control of my life.
Failure doesn't stop me, it teaches me.
I reach my goals with ease.
I get excited about my future.
I deserve amazing things.
I'm a kind, loving, compassionate person.

A day of positive labels

One grumpy man called me up following a seminar and told me that he applied the label *I feel good* to his life for one day. He must have said it to himself more than one hundred times throughout the day, he told me. To his surprise, he felt good. His boss noticed, his spouse noticed, even his dog seemed to follow him around more.

He laughed and said it was pretty impressive for a grumpy old man like him. I said, "Oh, you changed that label. You're not grumpy, you feel good."

I'd love for you, too, to spend an entire day applying positive labels to everything. From the moment you wake up, start labeling everything as good or progressively better. Whenever you can, bliss out on good feelings about these labels.

Try labels like

- Today is a great day.
- I feel good.
- I love taking a shower in the morning.
- It's great that I get to try tea because I ran out of coffee.
- Driving to work is so relaxing.
- I love it when it snows; it's so beautiful.
- I'm so excited to see this project through, despite the hiccups reaching the deadline.
- My work is meaningful.
- My colleagues are so helpful.
- My lunch hour is enjoyable.
- The sun is shining; it's a great day.
- These long meetings are a great way to uncover opportunities.
- My unhappy client means well; he appreciates working with me enough to show me how to strengthen our relationship.
- I remembered so many things today.
- I am so healthy.
- I feel so relaxed.

Notice each label is simple and feels easy. Naturally and easily accept these qualities; don't question or assess them. Labels just need to feel good.

If you complicate a label with your assessments, you are placing conditions on your happiness.

Just remember: you are after a feeling, not a goal.

· · · FEEL-GOOD HABITS · · ·

1   **Notice the way you feel.** Your emotions are always a barometer of whether you are going up or down. Emotions are simple to gauge. Do you feel good, or do you feel bad? If you feel good, you're moving forward. When you feel bad, you hold yourself back. A couple times a day, notice the way you feel: good or bad, happy or sad, up or down, neutral.

How do you know if you feel good or bad? You always know, you just have to pay attention. If you feel neutral or bad, intend to feel better. Don't assess why you feel bad, this would just put conditions on your feelings and make you feel worse. It will complicate your feelings because you will be dredging up the past. Instead, reach for a better thought or feeling. This may be as easy as labeling today as a good day.

2   **Raise your energy and vibration with positive emotions and affirmations.** Throughout the day, keep throwing positive thoughts and feelings at your life. Visualize positive circumstances, scenarios, and outcomes to projects. Sustain the uplifting feeling inside you for as long as you can.

3   **Bliss out on a positive label for a week.** To practice a high vibration, pick a positive label and bliss out on it for a week. For instance, you could label your work as fun. For the next week, keep perpetuating thoughts and feelings of fun about your job. Notice whenever you are having fun and revel in that feeling. When time flies by, you know you're having fun. So, appreciate the feeling and return to it a few times a day

for a week. Within a week you will have practiced a new, higher vibration, and your work will feel much more uplifting.

4 **Apply random positive labels.** Throw positive labels all over everything and everyone you observe for a day. Feel good about the labels, believe in them, because they don't have to prove themselves to you. They just have to feel good. Random feel-good labels help you appreciate life instead of tolerating it. Some examples of random positive labels:

- I love my dog.
- I adore my colleagues.
- My work is so rewarding.
- My mother is so kind.
- My spouse is so supportive

5 **Ditch the label.** What negative labels do you need to ditch? The annoying neighbor? The micromanaging boss? The wayward government? The bad economy? Lift the label by no longer giving it attention.

4

ELEVATE YOUR ENERGY AND VITALITY

FROM A FLICKER TO A ROARING FLAME

IN COLLEGE, I had a friend who was hit by a car. Insurance instantly paid out $5,000 to her. We thought she was so lucky.

Almost immediately, her luck changed. Now that she had extra cash, she dropped out of school. She was slapped with a $15,000 bill for her tuition. We did the math and realized she'd have to be hit by at least two more cars to afford that.

I fell out of touch with my uneducated friend, but I think of her often. Over the years, I've wondered whether luck is the invisible force that sends our life in one direction or another, or if we direct our fate.

When you're happy and you know it, your life will show it

Working behind the scenes is an invisible force that's shaping your life, one that is in your control. The invisible energy shaping your destiny is created by your thoughts and your emotions. It's not luck. Thoughts attract your reality.

Feeling good is easy; it's fun and almost whimsical. Let's take the easy route, bliss out, have fun, and enjoy our lives while we naturally get everything that we want. Let's celebrate positive good-feeling vibes. Let's nourish them all the time so we better understand what they are.

Good feelings are the key to your potential! There are many wonderful positive thought/feeling patterns you can bliss out on. Here are some of my favorites:

- Joy and happiness
- Love
- Prosperity and success
- Kindness and compassion
- Appreciation and gratitude
- Levity and fun
- Inspiration
- Relaxation and calm
- Optimism and hope
- Passion

Pick your favorite go-to good feelings, label them in your life, and bliss out on them often. Choose a couple right now. Focus on just one or two to begin with and get used to feeling these good feelings a lot. It doesn't matter what feeling you go to or how you label it, as long as it makes you feel good. Always go to the quickest, easiest way to bliss out on uplifting thoughts and feelings.

Throughout this book I talk a lot about happiness, but any positive thought will activate a positive vibration. They all work the same way, and they tend to work together.

Anytime you bliss out, you are simply bringing positive feelings into the present moment and enjoying the good vibes. With a bit of focused attention, they will expand, create a sustainable vibration, and build momentum.

Locating the good vibes

Where do we find these good vibes like joy, success, and compassion?

Right now, I want you to take your index finger and point it at your chest. Now lightly poke yourself in the middle of your chest, just below your collarbones. That's where the uplifting feeling of joy often starts. As you are poking around at your chest, remember this is where your good feelings reside—not in your bank account, on your iPhone, or on your social media wall—inside you.

The experience of an emotion results from the brain, heart, and body acting in concert. Positive emotion tends to radiate around your heart area and spread through your body. When you want to feel love, notice it unfold from the middle of your chest. Put your attention there and nurture loving feelings by thinking loving thoughts. Think about a puppy, a kind friend, or a good deed. With the help of your loving thoughts as a guide, love will swell up and expand.

Here's how to bliss out on positive feelings:

Put your *intention* toward a happy feeling. You can choose love, joy, gratitude—they all feel much the same way: good. If you intend to experience love, think loving thoughts not attached to any outcome. Next, you can mindfully focus your *attention* on the feelings of love in your chest. Don't judge or analyze them, just feel them. Use your loving thoughts to keep nurturing the feeling. Do this a few times a day, and pretty quickly you will start to see how powerful these good feelings are.

If you want joy, think joyful thoughts (intention) and focus on the feeling erupting in your chest (attention). Focus on it and nurture it as long as you can. Bliss out. Don't hold back on these uplifting feelings; they have been waiting for you and are key to your potential. Sustain that uplifting feeling inside you to practice that higher vibration. Soon it will flourish and attract more good feelings.

Regularly nourish positive thoughts and feelings inside you. Keep the focus in your chest without adding any external conditions to this bliss. You don't need anything from anyone to bliss out.

Breathe. Blissing out will be easy if you inhale a deep breath and let go of any tension or negativity with your exhale. Perpetuate your positive thoughts while you gulp up some deep breaths and let tension evaporate.

Positive emotion and vibration boost

To really bliss out, you need to stop conserving positive emotion and start using it. Now.

The origin and meaning of the word *emotion* is not far removed from *motion*. All emotions are either positive or negative energy or movement.

Raise your vibration and maintain it by consistently putting positive words, visualizations, energy, and enthusiasm inside you. Every time you focus on good-feeling thoughts, you are being mindful. It's one of the most important practices for your health and well-being.

From now forward, feel good as much as possible, no matter the circumstances. Keep turning over your positive labels, much like a song you keep singing to yourself and can't get out of your head.

Positive thoughts vibrate at a higher frequency inside you, that's why it feels good to bliss out. This frequency radiates

Bliss is not a doing, it's a state of being. **It's not a goal, it's a feeling.**

from you into your life. Happiness and other feel-good emotions are the raw materials to elevate you. Once you catch wind of joy, you take a new energetic path.

When I speak of elevating, I'm hinting at a vibration or frequency. I'm talking about an invisible energy current running through you at all times—a subtle vibration that is neutral but responds to thoughts, emotions, and actions.

When you raise your vibration, you can reach a blissful state of being. It's in the here and now, and it is vibrating through you.

Every thought has its own vibrational frequency. Positive thoughts vibrate at a higher frequency. Negative thoughts vibrate much lower. If you're predominantly negative, you may not notice a vibration at all. When you think positive, optimistic thoughts, you create powerful thought-frequencies. Some superbly optimistic days, you may feel like you're buzzing. It feels so good that you'll bliss out on these vibrations.

Your thoughts created this invisible vibration.

In other words, your thoughts translate into energy.

Although you can't see it, your thoughts and emotional vibrations are shaping your reality. In the world of quantum physics, like-energy attracts more like-energy and joins the current. If you focus on one area of your life and continue to think positive thoughts and spread high vibrations, you will start to see positive changes driven by the high frequency of your thoughts.

Everywhere you go, you are sensing people's vibration and they are sensing yours. All ideas are energy and are connected. We think with our whole body through our feelings, and these are powerful electromagnetic waves. Thoughts are a form of energy that carry a certain frequency and emit a vibration.

If we could all collectively lift our vibration, we would impact human consciousness. No pressure, but your thoughts can change the course of history.

Throw a party for your good vibes

My purpose here is to tempt you to think and feel positive because I know your uplifting emotions need an advocate. They are accustomed to being trampled on by stress.

I just love happy, fun, nothing-can-bring-me-down days, don't you? You feel unstoppable, like nobody can put their foot on your mood. You accomplish a lot, you do it with ease, and you feel so good.

Think about throwing a party. If you're having fun, the party gets better as the night progresses. Feel-good emotions build up momentum. All those positive thoughts and feelings propel you forward.

As you go about having fun and raising your vibration, remember any positive thought will do, just pick any thought/feeling that makes you feel happy. Don't analyze it or worry about it; it should be simple, easy, and fun. Just like a great party.

It's the forward positive momentum we are after, so any feeling that helps you get there works. It just has to be positive.

Fleeting good vibes

Everybody wants to feel good. I rarely meet people who actively promote to themselves a miserable life. Yet it's a lot more alluring to be grumpy than happy. Why is stress so compelling and joy so fleeting? Truth is, those feelings you were poking around at in your chest moments ago are short-lived. Temporary. That's why you have to consistently put happy feelings inside you and use your thoughts to keep replenishing them.

Why is happiness so elusive? So unreliable? It's here one moment and gone the next. It's like a fickle friend who shows up only when they feel like it. And then they only stick around until they have the itch to leave—and that's always too soon.

Joy is fleeting. Just like a salty bouillon cube dissolves in boiling water, our positive emotions dissipate. Bliss can be side-swiped by stress with one simple thought.

Happiness is fleeting. We want it to stick around, but it doesn't. It lacks grit.

Depicting happiness

And yet, happiness is unproblematic, undemanding, and uncomplicated. It has no goal and no expectations. It wants nothing from you but to make you feel good. It's subtle, non-seductive and unaggressive. It's short-lived and unassuming.

If only it would try harder. If only happiness could get its act together. Instead of aimlessly flowing, it should have some direction. Some meaningful purpose that persistently nags at you until you comply.

Happiness often seems wishy-washy and purposeless. It's easy to scowl at its mellow, accommodating, hassle-free ways.

Its carefree demeanor doesn't get your attention; it's not barking orders or using condescending words to lure you into action. It doesn't keep you on your toes like a demanding boss would. It's more like the generous and kind friend who loves you no matter what. It's a nice reassurance to have in your back pocket, but not a necessity.

Happiness is naive. It forgives. It doesn't judge, consider the facts, or reprimand you. It doesn't get attached to the environment. It's just there if you need it.

Happiness isn't demanding, so it doesn't command our attention. But stress does.

Depicting stress

Stress is guaranteed to get results. Stress isn't distributed with a dissolving flow and grace but with a feisty punch. It fires you up and pushes you. As you hustle around after your goals, you push your life around until it looks more favorable to you. It creates inner resistance and propels more stress.

The stress invested in reaching your goals has force, tenacity, and persistence. It's vigilant. Relentless. It hovers over your shoulder and reminds you of duty and struggle. Stress has its claws in you and motivates you to keep moving forward through fear. It has grit.

It's just doing its duty, helping you survive. Resistance helps you prepare to fight. Thousands of years of evolution has guaranteed stress as a motivational survival tactic. Happiness is just along for the ride.

Stress serves a purpose in the survival of our species, but happiness doesn't. The morbid reality is that feeling good is optional to our survival.

This isn't an abstract science lesson. It could be your life right now. The moment you roll aimlessly out of bed, happiness visits for a split second. Then your brain starts assessing your to-do list and stress commandeers your motivation and drive. As you go about your day, hunting for resolution to quell problems that irritate you, stress is there with you. It's in the background, chastising you to get things done. You pounce on problems to check off your to-do list, and fear, doubt, or worry are your guide. If this sounds like you, your thought/feeling vibration is low. You'll know by the way you feel—bad, irritated, bored, or neutral.

Happiness, joy, love, and all positive feelings are carefree and uncomplicated. **Feeling good is easy.**

Inviting happiness in

But good things happen in your life all the time. You reach a goal, deposit a paycheck, or receive kind words from your colleague. Feel-good emotions flow into you. You may temporarily feel elated, light, and joyful. Happiness is paying you a visit. Ask her to stay for a while. She has no demands or expectations, and she won't stay unless she's invited. Happiness will quickly dissolve in the presence of stress or demands.

Happiness wants nothing from you; you don't have to fix her or solve her problems. She just wants an invitation. Open the door and let her in. Be curious and enjoy her company.

For happiness to prevail, you need to remove all limitations and controls on her being inside you. This is the state of bliss.

Imagine someone invites you over and keeps frisking you for problems and pushing you to smarten up. Would you stick around? No? Well, happiness won't either.

Joyful feelings need repetition, a continuous replenishment. If you activate a high vibration and bliss out on it, maintaining it inside you for a while, this will be easy.

Happiness will never overstay her welcome, because stress is always waiting. Its vigilance will hold you in resistance and throw you back to your duty and chores. Goals and responsibilities will hijack these fleeting, happy moments. You have work to do. Problems to settle. Your hustle is in the background waiting to take over your performance routine.

The reason you need to remove the conditions and labels that bring you down is they create a resistance that smothers happiness. It can't exist in you as long as stress is there. Every time you stoke the fire and place happy thoughts and feelings inside you, you elevate your vibration. This positive frequency is the fuel that gives you forward momentum in your life.

AFFIRMATIONS FOR HAPPINESS

Happiness belongs to me.

I am happy.

I feel joy.

I'm stepping into my worthiness starting now.

Happiness is with me on my way.

I am aligned with love.

Everything is working out for me.

I create the life I desire with my good feelings.

My heart is full and content.

Life lights me up, with all its adventures.

I embrace joy and gently release everything that's not joy.

I love to bliss out on happiness.

How you became a fixer

Negative thoughts are potent. We hop from one to the next and they all come packed in a wallop of stress and urgency. Positive thoughts give you fleeting pleasure, but they don't coerce you with a climactic predicament. When stressful things happen, we feel compelled to expedite them. Fix them. When positive things happen, we briefly enjoy them and move on. When things go well, there's really nothing to do but to appreciate it. As long as things are going well, we don't have to change or improve. We stand still, but eventually without forward momentum we get stuck.

Take a moment to consider how stress is a motivational force in your routine. How often do you appreciate the glories of your life? Is your life tilted in favor of stress? For most people it is. When stress badgers you for attention, nominate happiness to take over. If you believe in her and want her as much as she wants you, she will.

Here's what you need to remember about all positive feelings: Happiness, joy, love, and all positive feelings are carefree and uncomplicated. Feeling good is easy.

Positive feeling is boundless. Unstructured. Limitless. It's far beyond what we can imagine. Perhaps this is our biggest beef with happiness. You can't define it, and it's unreliable. We can't dissect it and put it on a spreadsheet. It's not a goal; it's a feeling.

Joy is a flow, not a push. You don't convince it to obey. Instead, you invite it to the party.

Happiness doesn't take to your forced commands, but it does respond to open, warm invitations. You can't pin it down and force it to comply, but you can welcome it and bliss out on its energy.

You also can't bottle it to drink it in later. You don't need to—it's infinite, so you can never run out. The moment your mind starts commanding or containing it, happiness hides. It's not afraid; it's just waiting its turn.

Happiness and stress don't exist at the same time. They negate each other. You can't feel happy and sad simultaneously. You can't feel fearful and joyful at the same time. Negative and positive don't run through you at once. It's one or the other.

If you had only one space (your body), and happiness and stress had to fight for that space, who would win? Stress of course. It's the fighter. So, there you have it. Negativity and stress tend to rule our world because they are more potent, lasting, and punishing than happiness.

Joy inferno

Here's what we've been building up to: potential.

Your greatest asset is your focused good thoughts and feelings. Vibrant, buoyant, hopeful, effervescent good feelings glow in your chest and expand through you. Like stoking a fire, these feelings start as a flicker and through your attention to them become a roaring flame. The internal joy inferno you are building is an unwavering force that will transform your life.

When you bliss out in happiness it becomes a power source that will move you forward, transform you. Gleefully focus on stoking a joy inferno. Joy can't wait to transform your life.

Be happy in the now

Your brain is waiting to hear what you want. Tell it. Right now.

Happiness will spring into any moment you ask for it. Stop trying to put it off, and make joy a future date on your calendar. Use it now. You cannot force happiness on a timeline, but you can bring it into your present. Bliss is not a doing, it's a state of being.

Use simple routines, like the ones offered throughout this book—positive affirmations or visualizations, for example. These help you feel good and raise your vibration. Do them often. I use a happiness routine to let happy emotion get out in front of my day and build some forward momentum. Perhaps you will feel inspired to do the same.

Anytime something isn't going your way, you can invite happiness to guide you. Here's an example: I glanced at an email and felt immediately stuck in a conflict with a client trying to nail down a speaking engagement. We were unable to solidify a date because the COVID virus wreaked havoc on all our calendars.

I knew I needed to feel good to move forward before replying to my client. Feeling good always has to come first, so I used this quick visualization technique.

For a moment I stopped and thought about the upcoming speaking engagement. I imagined the audience, the huge ballroom, the dim lights, the lush velvet curtain behind the stage, and the podium off to the side, a fervent, bubbly anticipation and excitement in the room. The audience was cued up, inspired, and ready to move forward in their lives. I imagined the host introducing me. I felt overjoyed to spread inspiration throughout the ballroom. Good feelings were bouncing off the walls and lifting people up.

This vision made me feel good and, elevated in this way, I could reply to my client and help us both move forward, even though the circumstances remained sticky. Our goal was to solidify a date in the short term, which I knew right then we couldn't do. But my real goal was to feel good, and I can always do that.

With the flow of that feeling, my day moved forward and I accomplished a lot, with ease.

Your imagination sparks positive emotion

The anticipation of an event adds more to your happiness than the event itself. If you have a happy event in your calendar, like a vacation, dream about it. Bring the happy feelings about the future event into you now. Just like you can't force happiness, you can't guarantee that future events will deliver on the promised joy—but you can feel it now. If thinking about a future event or success makes you feel happy or prosperous, think about it. Feel it. Savor the feelings of joy as though they were happening now.

The event itself isn't as important as the feeling in you. You need those buoyant, boundless emotions. Live up to feeling good.

Our body doesn't know the difference between a real and imagined event. If the future event elevates your energy now, to your body it's real.

Anything you want in life, think about it; invite the elevated feelings into you and keep them as long as you can:

- Think and grow rich.
- Think and grow happy.
- Think and grow healthy.

It all starts with a thought and your feelings, which translate into a vibration.

Imagining and believing

Belief starts with a thought. Positive thoughts and emotions will uplift you and give you all the energy you need. Don't look to others to give you those thoughts. Put them inside you. Now. Feel how you want to feel. These self-assured, powerful thoughts and emotions are necessary to elevate you.

Your brain is so powerful. You can use visual images of success in your mind to help you build positive momentum in your life. Here's how it works. If you feel stuck in your career, imagine what you really want it to look like. If you desire a promotion, imagine yourself with that promotion. Label yourself as prosperous and bring the feelings of success inside you. You will feel elated, hopeful, powerful. Bliss out and sustain this vibration.

Imagine your office space, your colleagues, your customers all interacting with you in a positive way. Feel confident, alive, unstoppable. Sit in this vision of yourself for as long as it feels good.

Let your thoughts add details that inspire even more positive feelings. Don't throw in rules or doubt, just believe in your vision. If having your dog with you at work makes you feel good, add them into your vision. Even if your workplace currently has a no-dogs rule. Never limit yourself as you go about imagining

Joy is a flow, not a push. You don't convince it to obey. **Instead, you invite it to the party.**

and believing. You don't have to submit these dreams to HR. The whole purpose of this exercise is to create positivity in your career, and that forward momentum comes from these positive thoughts and feelings.

Now what if you don't get the promotion? I understand this is regrettable; however, you can recognize that you've already built so much positive momentum. You need to keep this going to prepare you for your amazing future.

If you feel disappointed, you'll need to lift the condition you placed on success. The condition is the promotion. You just need to find a way to feel good about not getting it. Look for a positive label for the experience. I would dance around the idea that there is a better opportunity around the corner. If you receive feedback with the rejection, look for any chance to grow in it. Be kind to yourself and the organization that denied you the opportunity. I'm sure it was a tough decision. You need to be relentless about feeling good about yourself and your job.

Watch your thoughts; any return to a feeling of failure or regret can start reversing your momentum.

If this promotion was a big deal to you, you will likely create a story about this experience. It's a story you will run around and tell everyone who will listen.

It could be the story of defeat, how you were mistreated, and how the organization fails to see value in its people. Or it could be a story about seeing your strengths, growing into your potential. It could be a story about a career that you love unconditionally.

You determine the story. Just know that whatever you label that story, good or bad, it will become true. The thoughts you keep thinking about that story become your belief, which becomes your reality.

Edit your environment

All the answers to your feelings are inside you, so be careful about noshing on negative information. Bad news or comparing yourself to others makes you feel bad, and you need to feel good to build positive momentum.

Go on a negative information diet. Your brain is susceptible to negative information. There are millions of people trying to offer you an elusive glimpse at happiness. Anytime you cling to outside sources like a pill, a plan, or a formula for hope, you may take yourself further from resolve. You are after inner resolve. It's inside you.

Stop chasing others' approval. Anytime you look outside yourself for others' blessings or support, you let their temperamental opinion matter more than your own. Know your worth. When you look to others for validation or signs of significance, you weaken yourself. They don't know you. You know you. People aren't watching you, they're feeling you. When you feel good, they feel good about you. You can't feel good by needing other people to feel good about you. Simplify your life by lifting any condition that other people need to approve of you.

Resist the temptation to gorge on impulsively evil news feeds. Don't scan Instagram, unconsciously soaking up people's fake lives. Your nervous system is sensitive to fake or negative news, which fires up stress.

Instead, find some Instagrammers to tell you positive stories. Follow YouTube stars who found their fame from finding themselves. Look for people whose success feels good and doesn't hinge on others' approval. If you sniff the scent of an ego, leave.

Be relentless. Only accept messages of hope and inspiration. If a source of information makes you sad, fearful, jealous, or upset. Stay away. It's instigating stress.

You may need to cut people out of your life. Negative people spewing negative messages will hold you back. You are only connected to them through worry and stress. Fear and worry are your bonds. You have both built up a negative point of attraction toward certain depleting topics. Do you regularly like to complain about workloads? Or ineffective leadership? Or the government? Because you return to these topics often and they make you feel bad, they build up a strong negative magnetic charge. These negative topics become so activated in you that you feel compelled to keep returning to them. No bond is greater than two co-workers who hate the same thing.

Your stress cycles love how you fire each other up and perpetuate the fury. But it makes you feel crummy.

You're letting go of this. You won't need them. You need to diligently stay away from these negative people and topics until you lift their negative charge. Once you give these thought patterns a break, you deactivate these feelings. Eventually, you can go back to these people and topics and they won't have the same depleting power over you.

Instead, start asking your life for what you want and put it in you right now.

If you want health, tell yourself you're healthy. It's not a lie. Even if a physical illness is in you right now, health is here, too, or you wouldn't be alive. Nurture health, not illness. Climb out of illness and into a healthy life.

If you don't think and believe in your health, vibrant health will always be something you wish for but never have.

If you want success, tell your brain about your success. Give it specific details if it helps you feel your success. All you need to do is pull the success out from inside you by instigating its feeling right now. Live in it for a moment. Bliss out on success and keep inviting it back.

Or you can just keep regurgitating thoughts about your failure and lack of success. It's up to you.

··· FEEL-GOOD HABITS ···

1   **Plan days of happy labels.** Below are adjectives that describe different qualities of happiness. They are all feelings, so please feel them rather than analyzing them or making them a goal. If you want to bliss out on these good-feeling labels, you just need to sustain that positive vibration inside you longer. Choosing from the list below, label your day with an adjective that makes you feel happy. If you label your day as bouncy, you might leap out of bed, have a spring in your step, and bounce around your office. You hurdle through your to-do list, getting stuff done. Use a different label every day. Have fun with them, and spend time with different flavors of labels on different days, as each will show you another side of happiness. And remember, although any of these labels could be perceived as goals, the point here is to focus on feelings of happiness:

ACCEPTANCE, GO WITH THE FLOW

Easy	Satisfying	Curious	Enjoyable
Agreeable	Calm	Light	Serene
Content	Carefree	Fluid	Delightful
Freeing			

UPLIFTING

Expansive	Jovial	Joyful	Fun
Cheerful	Jolly	Blissful	Bouncy

HERE AND NOW

| Wistful | Giddy | Frolicking |
| Fleeting | Gleeful | Flirty |

ENERGIZING

Buzzing	Big	Optimistic
Thrilling	Beaming	Enthusiastic
Exciting	Peppy	Sunny

PURPOSE AND PROSPERITY

| Passionate | Rewarding |
| Inspired | Successful |

2 **Cut out social media and news for a week.** It won't kill you, I promise. I notice how social media makes me feel, and most of the time, it's not self-affirming. When you go back to Facebook, Instagram, TikTok, or your platform of choice, notice how different posts make you feel. If a source is negative, cut it off.

Never post things on social media looking for approval. It will be challenging because the whole thing hinges on you mindlessly affirming whether people like you. I have a rule. When I post on social media, I don't go back and look at it for twenty-four hours. By this time, any attachment I might have to others' approval has faded. Structure your time on social media so it won't continually bring you down. Before posting anything, ask yourself, *Am I posting this hoping for approval?* If so, reaffirm to yourself you don't need anyone's approval. Do things because they're meaningful to you, not to get others' approval.

3   **Fill your day with positive thoughts.** Imagine you are given one hundred positive thoughts a day, and you need to use them all up. Let your thoughts revolve around positive labels. You can generate the same positive thought over and over again, or several different uplifting ones, and you cannot end the day without speaking about them, thinking them, writing them, or infusing your behaviors with them.

4   **Go for the good vibes.** I suggest you develop a few go-to routines that put good-vibe feelings inside you. The more you repeat them, the more they will reward you with blissed-out feelings and instant positive momentum. Just remember to focus on the vibrant feelings, not the doing. Don't complicate this with rules or agendas. Here are a few ideas:

Grooving to funky music: Put on some happy, fun, groovy songs that you can dance along with. Be a bit goofy; this is not a choreographed routine. You are not trying to look good, you're just having fun, for no reason at all. Feel the zest of a lively lyric vibrate through you, and let the good feeling spread into your day.

Isn't it great how...: Use the phrase "Isn't it great how..." over and over in your day. It will prompt you to always be on the lookout for great things happening around you.

Visualization: Quick, fun visualizations are great. Use them often—before going into a meeting or doing a task that you find draining, while you're on the subway, or standing in a line. Without any attachment to outcome, imagine great things happening to you. Keep it short. Get in and get out. Don't complicate it with deadlines or goals. Just feel good. Go back to the same vision often to build a positive point of attraction.

Vision board: Regularly cut out pictures of things that you like and place them on a wall you look at often. Choose photos of anything that makes you feel good: cars, planes, fun destinations, horses, beautiful homes or interiors. Look at these pictures often and simply enjoy how they make you feel.

Compassion: The go-to feelings when life is hard are kindness and self-compassion. Cultivating these will offer relief when times are tough. When work or life is harassing you, think about how the wider circumstances are challenging and how everyone is struggling. Don't get tough on yourself, get compassionate with yourself. Have some understanding for what you're going through. It's not your fault, everyone would have a hard time with this. Be nice to yourself just like you would be to a struggling friend.

Laughter: Laughing boosts endorphins and makes you feel good. It helps you take yourself lightly and this vibrancy bounces off stress. It's also one of the least complicated ways to feel good. You can simply laugh for no reason at all and start to feel better. Again, focus on the feeling of fun and levity. You don't have to make big plans that will cause you to laugh. You don't need to glean good jokes from the internet or become a comedian. Just laugh, it's simple.

5

SEEK POSITIVE MOMENTUM

LET LIFE FLOW IN THE DIRECTION YOU WANT

FROM TIME to time I join the ranks of the lunch hour hustle of downtown commerce. It's always revealing. I find myself shoulder to shoulder with mobs of people, rushing from point A to point B. We are all busy and focused on getting to our destination. While we hustle to work, we shovel our lunches in our mouths, never appreciating the food's texture or taste.

Our bodies are moving forward but our brains are wrapped up in thoughts of deadlines and to-do lists. Clues of our inner resistance are revealed in the tension in our jaw and the strain crawling around our shoulders. During the workday, even lunch can be complicated, yet it is meant to be enjoyed.

The momentum of this lunch hour routine is hinged on aggravated goals. Goals are all about future timelines and deadlines, not about what's happening right now. Eating should be enjoyable, but stress presses the pause button on happiness.

The moment you complicate happiness, you lose it and head toward stress. Anytime you feel bad, you know you are complicating your life with depleting thoughts and feelings.

I want you to gain a better appreciation for how you feel. Once you sniff a wobbly disposition inside you spurred on by stress, you will learn to dissolve it with appreciation, self-compassion, and joy. You will learn to uncomplicate negative, complex thoughts with fun, easy, positive ones.

Of course, it's normal to feel sad or angry—the liquor industry is built on it. Just don't wallow for too long. Eventually you need to move forward.

Your "work" now, such as it is, is to nourish those good-feeling emotions inside you, but—more importantly—to help you build positive momentum. Bliss out with the repetition of happy thoughts, and not only will it make you feel good, it will propel you forward.

You are after this positive momentum, not just an occasional positive thought. Steady repetition of good thoughts and feelings is key.

In the previous chapter, we explored how happiness is a boundless, flowing, fleeting feeling that's just around for the good vibes. It's simple. It's easy. Stress is difficult. It's hard, complicated, and lasting. Happiness isn't. But it is short-lived.

Goal-free happiness

All positive emotions are uncomplicated. They are light, easy, flowing, and fulfilling. You don't need to barter with them, manipulate them, or try to capture them for later. You just have to enjoy being happy. It's simple. Your real goal is no goal. It's just to feel good. As long as you can just sit and bliss out on happy emotions, you are on track. You will move forward.

If negativity and conflict are absorbing your attention like a sponge, you need relief. Your life is too complicated. I get how stress creates resistance and compels you to fix your life, but this goal-oriented, hustle-driven environment makes it impossible for happiness to appear for very long. It will always get trampled on by stress. This conflict and negativity is what holds you back.

Get out in front of your day with joy

Line up with what you want before you act. I suggest that for a moment every morning, ditch your goals and just be in happiness. Reach for the best happy thought/feeling combination you can and just stay there feeling good for as long as you can. Let joy flow through you like a current.

Very quickly you will be able to suss out your happy feelings early on in your day and let those loose to flow into whatever you do. Next, throw happiness at your goals. Instead of jumping into your to-do list where joy may be a byproduct, lead your day with joy. Imagine the situations and goals ahead of you today working out well. Infuse thoughts of your day with anticipation of happiness, fun, optimism, and flow.

This is living from the inside out. Joy, appreciation, love, or any happy feeling comes first. Then you go after your goals. Because happiness is easy and fun, it will start your day off in an easy, enjoyable way. If this is how you feel, you know you're going in the right direction.

Ultimately, you want to get a grip on your energy momentum. If you can start your day happy and keep this intention alive, you will gather a distinct momentum. Build up enough good days with positive momentum and your entire life springs toward the life that you want.

Positive momentum—basking in appreciation for life

If your energy is positive, it moves forward into your day. It flows easily and time tends to fly by. You feel good and things happen effortlessly. If you are in a place in life where you are content and happy, you have a lot of positive momentum. On the surface, you like your life; it looks good to you. You love your job, house, children, spouse. Your thoughts are predominantly positive, and you have a lot of appreciation and gratitude for everything and everyone.

You may think life feels good because it looks good on the surface—you have a great job, wonderful kids, and a loving spouse. Why wouldn't you be happy? But it's the other way around. You didn't wake up one day with a great life. Instead, your predominantly positive thoughts and feelings gave you momentum that developed into a life that you want.

Those positive, easy, flowing good feelings are your predominant vibe. You look forward to everything and you often bask in appreciation for your life. You rarely feel stalled or stuck because your energy keeps moving you forward. Because that energy is positive it's easy, lightweight, and uncomplicated. It doesn't drag you down or hold you back. Somehow you can always skim over stress and find your happiness. It doesn't mean you don't deal with dilemmas or conflict, it just means you do it with ease. You never wrestle with difficult circumstances. Instead your positive blissful vibes help you keep life simple. The positive feelings propel you forward.

Positive feelings seep into conflict in your life and detach you from the complexity. A light, buoyant, blissful feeling teases out the negative, draining intensity of stress and makes everything easier. It playfully pokes at stress and lightens its load.

If you have positive momentum, it means you don't just occasionally shoot positive thoughts and feelings at your life. You have created a positive force that drives you forward. It's not transactional; it is pervasive and propels you toward more good things.

This momentum is constantly climbing forward into your life. It's not a hustle, it's a flow.

The reason relationships always start off great in the beginning is both partners are on the lookout for positive aspects of

You don't have to be the bellwether of bad news. **Instead, tune in to positive potential.**

the other person. You can always keep this spirited optimism alive by continually pointing out the positive aspects of everything and everyone in your life.

"Stuckness"

Momentum means movement. Your life picks up momentum through your thoughts, feelings, and actions. The direction is up to you.

If you feel like your life isn't going anywhere, you are stuck. In this neutral territory, you can quickly head backward. You may look around at your life, your job, house, spouse, and feel neutral, bored, possibly apathetic. They are only *okay*. Your life is a drag.

In other words, you haven't decided what direction you will take. And you look at your life to evaluate how it will perform. You attach your prognosis. If life surprises you and outperforms your expectations, you feel good, and maybe even build some positive momentum.

More likely, when things go wrong, the intensity of the negative feelings will pull your momentum backward and you'll enter negative territory.

Negative momentum—tumbling in reverse

If, for you, life tends to be difficult and complicated, you've likely built up negative momentum. Most things are stressful, and you tend to fight, to push life around. Life relentlessly presents problems you must fix. You tend to label your life with disappointment, worry, and regret. You question yourself and others, and your life seems complicated.

Stress has won the battle. It has commandeered your performance and will persuade you to further complicate your life. The complexity of stress makes life tenuous and uncertain. It drags your thoughts into past mistakes and chastises you and instills fear for your future. You move from tedious and annoying stuck feelings toward a more worrisome, angry, and fear-inducing existence.

That's because you left neutral territory, where you had grown annoyed with feeling stuck, and your momentum started backing up. Like a car in reverse, you are pulled back by worry and doubt.

This isn't the result of a few bad thoughts. It is a negative momentum that picks up speed and complicates your life. All negative thoughts are complex, heavy, resistant. If you continue to return to them, they will gather the momentum to push you back and away from your life.

Turning around your momentum

The last thing I want you to do is beat yourself up if you have recognized negative momentum in your life. You want to turn negative and complex into positive, simple, fun, and uplifting. If you do, through the help of a few feel-good habits, you will discover the delight of moving forward.

Do not take this on like it's a physics project. Happiness is something you have, not something you work for. You won't be assessing happiness or mapping it on a spreadsheet. The more you can take your momentum lightly the easier it will be to propel it forward.

To go from negative to positive momentum, you need to uncomplicate your life. You may think this means simplifying your circumstances—getting rid of the condescending girlfriend and quitting the demoralizing job. This is tempting, but be careful not to complicate your life even further. Instead, recognize that your invisible thoughts and feelings have created any backward momentum. The more you focus on negative thoughts, the more complex and righteous they become. They drain your energy.

To reverse this momentum, steadily invest your attention into uplifting, positive thoughts and feelings. Think of this as easy and fun. Go about it lightly to tease apart the complexity of your thoughts. Start noticing the positive aspects of your life, even if they are small and simple (usually they are).

If you have a lot of negativity, you'll have to start with forgiveness, self-compassion, and kindness. You can only move forward when you forgive your past. This will only be difficult if you are focused on effort rather than good feelings. Just trust and focus on feeling better. Label forgiveness and kindness on everything and everyone (including yourself). Feel the relief. Letting go of what you've been carrying around for so long will feel delicious. Eventually you can imagine yourself floating through your day with playfulness and ease. You are after a light, buoyant, energized feeling.

Cling to gratitude—for your job, your car, or any part of your life. Even if your car breaks down, think about how it was a great car; it has been good to you. You want to treat it well and fix it up.

Reach for any scrap of appreciation you can find. If you have a predominantly negative perspective, you need to broaden its limits with appreciation. Widen your perspective past the angle your doubts habitually place. Create a habit of randomly appreciating things around you in a very easy, uncomplicated way. Choose something random but pleasing to appreciate. Pick something you don't have to buy—a flower or a light snowfall—something just there in front of you, as it has always been. The smaller and less attached you are to it, the better. It's less complicated.

See if you notice a good feeling swirl around in your chest while looking at and appreciating small, simple things. Take the easiest, simplest label or thought/feeling you can find. ("I love my yard." "My job is fun." "I adore the sun shining on me.") If this feels hard, difficult, or draining, you're complicating it. Appreciate simple things, like a cup of coffee or a smile from a stranger. Pay attention to any happy feelings that explode inside you.

Anytime you catch yourself feeling bad, notice you are choosing complex, judgmental, negative thoughts. Knowing these thoughts aren't helping you, abandon them if you can. Remember that all positive emotion is fleeting; it won't stay for long. This is why you need the repetition. Keep pumping positive intention, thoughts, and feelings into your day.

It can be fun and easy to turn your momentum around, and it is going to take a lot of repetition to fuel your direction forward. Eventually you will be able to bliss out in a higher vibration for a sustained period.

Can you add as well as you subtract?

Right now you're really good at picking things apart and finding their deficiencies, but can you add as well as you subtract? To turn your momentum around, you'll need to invite positive, expansive thoughts in too. Look at life for its opportunities. You don't have to be the bellwether of bad news. Instead, tune in to positive potential.

Negativity is always a zero-sum game: you subtract everything until there's nothing left. Uplifting thoughts add to and broaden your perspective. You naturally consider expanding your options.

Take Clara, for example, whose boss was micromanaging her. That was annoying because she knew she was better at her job than he thought she was. Perhaps you can see, though, that

Stress is complex, but happiness is **as simple as one plus one.**

carrying this line of thought along would only make Clara's situation more complex and challenging. She would assess why she's right and he's wrong. She would doubt herself and her job. She may think her only option is to hustle and prove herself, subtracting any expansive thinking from her experience.

But what if she reached for a better feeling, broadening her perspective beyond her thoughts of strangling her boss? What if she considered the pressure her manager was under, recognizing the struggles that they shared? If she focused on the fact that they both wanted the same thing and reminded herself of the rewards of her job, how might her situation change?

Recognizing her negative spiral, Clara chose to be grateful for her career and all the opportunities the job offered her, plus the rewards of impacting her industry.

Wide-open, positive thoughts will always help you find balance. Once you lift the resistance of negative feelings, you can really fly forward.

A life inventory of momentum

You can have positive, stalled, or negative momentum in different areas of your life. Some areas or relationships may be moving forward while others may be stalled or moving backward.

Take an honest look at your momentum. Overall, which direction are you moving in? How do you know? By the way you feel. If you generally feel good in your life, you have a wind at your back helping you along. If you feel negative or stuck, you may feel like you are pedaling a ten-speed bicycle into a gale-force headwind. You just need to simplify your perspective and release resistance to different areas where your emotions are negative or stuck.

Evaluating different areas of your life may help. Try this.

Feel-good area/positive momentum

Choose one area of your life that feels good (for example, a relationship, a job, your health, your home, religion, diet, and so on). This is an area you have already built up positive momentum. Write it at the top of a page and, underneath, list words that describe how it feels to you. For instance, your relationship with your spouse may feel rewarding, loving, easy, fun, engaging, playful, understanding, supportive.

These feelings are helping you move forward in life together. Your spouse is easy to be with, you make decisions easily and move forward with no conflict. You find yourselves getting closer every day. Life with your spouse is uncomplicated and it feels good.

Review your list and revel in the feeling of easy, fun momentum. You want this ease and flow in all areas of your life—and you can have it. You just have to build the same positive momentum in every part of life.

Stuck momentum

Now write about an area in life where you are stuck. Perhaps it is a project you are working on that keeps getting stalled. That project might be annoying, irritating, apathetic, boring, and so on.

Consider how you can build positive momentum. You need to decide to feel good about the project. Stuck is susceptible, so don't take cues from your environment about how to feel. Look forward, not backward. Don't hold a grudge, throw a party and celebrate even the smallest milestones. Imagine things going well; see everyone involved as doing the best they can. Reach for any thought that makes you feel good. Hint: these thoughts should be simple and easy, and they should look forward at a positive future not backward, blaming the past. They add rather than subtract.

With the help of a few simple feel-good habits, you can catch wind of a positive feeling vibration, sustain it. Bliss out on it.

Negative momentum

Finally, choose an area in your life where you have built up negative momentum. How do you identify that? It makes you feel bad. In life you try to avoid these people or situations. They drain you. For example, let's say you choose a person you have conflict with. It's not bad blood between you; it's bad thoughts and feelings. Write down the words to describe these relationships. You might feel anger, regret, worry, doubt, resentment, and so on.

Look at these words and own that you have complicated these relationships with your muddled thoughts and feelings. You may believe it's their fault, but the whole thing is holding you back. You need to nudge your thoughts and feelings in a positive direction. Anytime you give over to a negative thought about this person, you move backward. Forgive negative thoughts and keep reaching for positive ones. Don't take yourself too seriously about it all.

Forgive yourself and your enemy. It may not be easy at first, but don't make it harder than it needs to be. The positive emotions you seek are simple.

Instead of labeling this person as your *enemy*, choose a positive word. Perhaps *detailed*, *diligent*, or *helpful* fits. You know if the label works by the way you feel. For instance, you may decide to label someone you despise as *kind*. But your gut tells you they are not kind, and the label feels wrong. But could you call them *tenacious*? Or maybe *committed*? Or *loyal*? Or *reliable*? Find a good quality that feels right. Use that label until you can massage it into happier territory.

Eventually, you'll find your way to feeling small amounts of gratitude for their efforts or skill. You'll appreciate the past you've had together, the lessons you've learned. Pretty soon, whenever you butt heads in conflict, you'll open up to their perspective as opportunity. Now your relationship will start to move forward. You are building positive momentum in your life.

And if you can build up enough positive momentum, you will be unstoppable.

Develop feel-good habits with this same mental routine with all people or situations that you have negative emotions toward. Just keep reaching for thoughts and feelings that lift you up and give you relief; keep imagining what you want and building up positive emotion about this area of your life.

Along the way remind yourself how powerful this mindset is—you are reversing negative momentum that has been holding you back.

Whenever you sense you've ignited a higher vibration, sustain it. Bliss out as long as you can to practice this high vibration.

More feel-good habits to turn around momentum

When you read about and do the activities below, you may be tempted to brush them off because they are so basic. If they seem simple, though, this means you are doing things right.

Delirious appreciation

Appreciation unattached to circumstances is a strong habit. When you stop and notice something beautiful around you, it can unleash a blissful radiance inside you. The goal is to feel good as often as you can; random appreciation is a credible way to get there.

My favorite way to bliss is through random but continual appreciation. Choose something simple in front of you to adore for a while. Adore it. Feel good about it. Notice its color, shape, and texture. That's it. What you're really doing is activating a higher-frequency vibration. With enough attention to the positive, it will catch on fire and move you forward. You are activating a curiosity that sees things not for what they are but from a perspective of greater potential.

You can always lift your emotions through appreciation. Even when life disappoints, hidden beneath your complex perspective is something to cherish. For instance, angry clients are hard, but if you open to their feedback they may be pointing you in the direction of opportunities to easily improve. If you appreciated their perspective and saw this potential, your business could catapult forward, your relationship with your client would also move forward, and you would feel good.

Love

I knew my ex-husband deserved to be happy—but I married him anyway. Eventually I realized the only person responsible for my happiness is me.

Real love is unconditional. The conditions you place on your love keep it at arm's length. Practice thinking about someone you love. Think about their smile and their good qualities. Now send them love through your thoughts. Wish them well in life, imagine them being happy and content. Imagine your relationship flourishing. Remember, none of this is attached to any sort of goal or outcome—it's a feeling. It's inside you and doesn't require anything from anyone to feel good.

Anytime you feel disappointment toward someone you love, pinpoint the condition you are placing on love (for example, she must listen to me, he doesn't appreciate me, they are not supportive). Lift this condition if you can. Next, start tapping (or rest your hand on) your chest. This may seem odd, but it is a reminder to look for love in all the right places—inside you. Nurture feelings of love inside you for that person. Appreciate their good qualities and wish them love. Feel compassion for your loved one and yourself, as your relationship is under some strain. Give your partner the benefit of the doubt and assume that they mean well. Remind yourself of their good qualities. Through massaging these thoughts you will be able to find lighter, less resistant thoughts about your relationship and your partner. Eventually, you will get back to positive-feeling territory with passion, love, and appreciation.

Keep up the positive thoughts and feelings and you will build forward momentum in your relationship. Once you have enough forward momentum, your relationship will be so strong nothing can rock it.

Pay attention to the light, hopeful feelings in your chest—this is love. It's one of the most powerful emotions around.

Visualization for success and prosperity

Most ambitious people are after success. Inside you is a strong desire to succeed. While success looks different to everyone, it shares one quality: it's a feeling inside. Successful feelings are light, buoyant, optimistic, and hopeful.

Feelings of success can move you forward as long as they aren't hinged on conditions. The moment you attach this drive to other peoples' approval and specific outcomes, it can be depleting. Start with the feeling, and the success can more easily flourish in your life.

Create for yourself a visualization of success. Imagine your success with just enough detail to feel good about it. You can imagine making lots of money, having lots of amazing customers, living in a nice home. It doesn't require you to make the money right now or buy the home. It's just the feelings of prosperity you're after. If it is simple, easy, and feels good, the visualization is working. Bliss out on it to practice this feel-good vibration.

This is not goal-setting. This vision of success will go along nicely with your goals to keep you primed for prosperity; however, it's not hinged on achieving goals. Through visualizing pictures of success in your brain, just reach the best blissful feeling about success you can find and sustain it for as long as you can. Enough perpetual thinking in this direction will build positive momentum.

Happiness starts as a flicker **and through your attention to it becomes a roaring flame.**

For example, Jerry wants to start a consulting business. A great visualization for him would be imagining himself with a booming business. He could add details like clients signing contracts and giving him deposits; he can imagine clients thriving from his advice, and himself feeling content and satisfied with his business. As Jerry gets lost in these wonderful visualizations, his only goal is to feel really good about his success. This will fuel the momentum to boost his consulting business.

Ride the wave

Always ride the wave of momentum when it swells in your life. Even small things that go well are showing you positive momentum. The longer you relish the good feelings, the more you launch forward motion in life.

You can ride on the coattails of someone else's momentum. If someone has a lot of great stuff going on, you can contribute your own positive spin on it. It will be great to just feel like you're moving forward—this is the feeling you want.

If you're stuck, you can remember previous good times where your life was going well and bring that momentum back just by remembering it. However, if this feels complicated because it creates doubt, abandon this approach. It has to feel good to work.

Just take it light and easy, you can't go wrong as long as you feel good.

··· FEEL-GOOD HABITS ···

1   **Complete the inventory of your life's momentum.** Return to the section "A life inventory of momentum" on page 123 and continue to evaluate areas in your life where you are stuck or moving backward. Follow the steps to begin nudging your thoughts and feelings toward the positive.

2   **Visualize with bliss.** Pick an area in your life where you persistently set goals (exercise, work, home). Take a moment to see that area of your life for what it is right now. Appreciate what you do and where you're at without any goal attached to it. Then notice what your attachment to your goal feels like. Is it a heavy, sinking feeling or does it give you energy? Change your story and predominant thoughts about your goals. For instance, label the experience of losing weight as fun and rewarding. Gradually focus on good thoughts and feelings and build positive momentum in any area of your life. Keep a general focus and imagine just enough detail to feel good in your visualization.

3   **Keep gently guiding happiness into your life.** Write out your positive affirmations daily and feel the affirmative words linger inside you. Bliss out on these good feelings several times a day and sustain the good feelings in you for as long as you can.

4   **Every day, write a list of things you are grateful for and why.** Remember gratitude and appreciation build curiosity and a more expansive perspective.

In this gratitude practice you might jot down things like

- I am grateful for my dog because they show me unconditional affection.

- I am grateful for the spruce tree in my backyard because its beauty reminds me of my strength.

- I am grateful for my job because it allows me to have a great lifestyle.

As always, the way you feel is most important. Put the feelings of gratitude inside you as you write. Bliss out and sustain feelings of gratitude for as long as it feels right.

5 **Get out in front of your day with a positive feeling of momentum.** First thing in the morning, start imagining things going well; imagine feeling good. Affirm to yourself words like, *Today will be a great day! I feel so good!* Blissing out is easiest in the morning because any negativity or stressful thoughts took a break while you slept.

6 **Line up with your decisions.** All day long you make decisions, small and large. Before and after you make a decision, line up with it by thinking good thoughts about it. Never make a decision and then build up mental anguish by doubting it.

6

TAKE IT EASY

COMPASSION IS A GAME CHANGER

AN EXPERIENCE that taught me self-compassion remains emblazoned on my brain like a tattoo. I was in my early thirties and performing stand-up comedy. It was new material, which is always scary. Every comedian knows that untested punchlines can destroy a meaningful career. The comedian up before me had killed it. He was a triumphant success. The whole audience embraced him like a long-lost fraternity brother.

When it was my turn onstage, I was already tense because I felt I had to outdo the next Jim Carrey. I tenuously approached the spotlight. I peered out at the crowd, and they looked back at me with the collective glare of a disappointed schoolteacher. Every punchline I threw out fell flat. The audience members shifted uncomfortably in their seats, shooting disapproving looks around the room.

I could feel my inner critic pounce on me from the shadows. Self-doubt overwhelmed me, eating me up from the inside out. I started mentally berating myself with self-defeating words. The situation was getting desperate.

Then I locked eyes with a woman two rows back. She was sitting next to a very large, angry man with huge biceps. Her face was puffy and red, and I could see lines of tears glistening on her cheeks. She looked sad, lonely, and defeated. I felt a sudden, unexpected wave of compassion unleash inside me. I genuinely hoped that whatever was dragging her into fear and sadness, she wouldn't be too hard on herself. I felt the urge to leave the stage and go to her, hug her, and tell her everything was going to be okay.

That's when I felt it. Instantly, the pressure inside me subdued. The fleeting feelings of kindness for a stranger were enough to give me relief from my nasty self-critic. I removed the imaginary knife from my throat and realized the pain I was putting myself through. My inner upheaval instantly subsided.

I looked out at the crowd and realized they were all suffering and in pain, too. The whole reason they were here was to forget about it for a while. In an instant our shared human struggle created a magical bond. This room full of scathing enemies became my family. It was like something unlocked in me, and my whole demeanor changed from attached and needy to compassionate and grateful. All my jokes were the same, but they landed differently with the audience as my self-aggression softened.

The audience eased up and laughed with me. I spend the next ten minutes throwing out punchlines, unattached to the laughter but finding levity in the tragedy and joy of life with strangers for a while.

In the bigger picture I could see the cause of my upheaval wasn't the audience, the outstanding comedian before me, or even mediocre jokes. It was me. I had created the struggle by being hard on myself.

Does your hustle mean you're hard on yourself?

One of the reasons we are compelled to hustle is because we feel we need to outdo others. We need to look good and outperform everyone else. Our productivity is a badge of honor. But this only props up our ego, not authentic good feelings.

Most people have been taught that strength comes from being tougher, more confident, or better than others. It doesn't. Real power springs from compassion. Kindness and compassion love you no matter what. Unconditional love allows you to soften and lift conditions that prevent your happiness and success.

Instead of creating separation and trying to outdo others, compassion mends certainty into the fabric of our shared being. Putting others down to build yourself up can never move your life forward. In the short term, stirring up conflict may help you get what you want, but if that is at the expense of others, everyone loses.

Shauna Shapiro's work on compassion shows that kindness allows us to move forward and learn because it bathes us with dopamine, turning on the learning centers of the brain. When we feel shame or judgment, the center of the brain that relates to growth and learning shuts down. In other words, self-judgment, hustling, and being hard on yourself and others does not lead to self-improvement.[5] Compassionate thoughts allow you to see stress for what it is and still grow. These thoughts might sound like

- Everything will be okay.
- Struggling is normal.
- It's not your fault. If you messed up, you didn't do it on purpose.
- Things don't always go as planned.
- You are not the core of the conflict.
- Circumstances change, and you can't control them.

Kind, compassionate thoughts help you see potential, create understanding, and move forward. They cradle uncertainty and help you grow. You need the loving acceptance of compassion to

Self-kindness doesn't tell you not to be upset; **it soothes you when you are. It creates acceptance.**

get there; otherwise you may just disregard others' perspectives and limit growth.

Negative assessment of others is complex and draining. It always stalls you. Yet so many people have been taught that we need to outthink, outsmart, and outdo others. These types of hard assessments create distance between others and yourself. As long as you have to be good and others have to be worse, there is not much room for joy. This perspective also forces you to look for the weakness in others, which can never make you feel good. Ever. It's just the wrong energy vibration. It's limiting, not expanding.

Compassion and kindness are middle-zone feelings. When life causes you to struggle, compassion and kindness are the helping hands that pull you into a positive feelings zone.

Self-kindness doesn't tell you not to be upset; it soothes you when you are. It creates acceptance.

Here's an example of what can happen without compassion. My friend is a life coach. She has created a thriving business and has lots of clients. But she recently threw in the towel and completely walked away from her coaching practice. I asked her why.

She said it was exhausting listening to people's problems all day long. She felt annoyed and frustrated hearing people constantly complain. She tried to guide them forward, but so many people just refused to give up their resentment and anger. In fact, the whole reason they came to her for coaching was because they wanted somebody to listen to them complain. Nobody else would; they had also grown tired of the bellyaching.

It's hard being a coach when all you do is talk about people's problems. This just activates these negative thoughts and keeps them alive. It's rarely helpful to regurgitate painful experiences from the past. People need to move forward. If her clients had been able to embrace self-compassion and kindness, perhaps my friend's coaching practice would still be alive. Kindness and compassion never pretend hardship doesn't exist, but they also ensure you move forward and don't get stuck in the past.

Compassion reaches around struggling thoughts and nudges them forward. It lifts hard assessments of life by showing understanding for others. Compassion isn't about justifying who's wrong or right, it's just about appreciation and understanding. It turns conflict into potential because it expands to include all perspectives.

Judgment limits your perspective, compassion helps it grow. It's about potential.

Also, the longer you focus on problems, the harder it is to let them go. It keeps these negative assessments activated in you. Only positive emotion moves anyone forward, and having some understanding and compassion for yourself and others in struggle would give so much relief.

Letting go of your past when it is a quagmire of complex emotions is hard. Complex thoughts and feelings hold you in the past and get more and more complicated the longer you entertain them. Every time you return to thoughts of misery, they are activated and grow stronger. The trouble is, denying and repressing emotions only makes things worse. Pretending everything is okay means it isn't.

So, how can we get our direction right and move forward when we have so much emotional baggage?

Through compassion, kindness, and forgiveness. These positive emotions throw understanding, nurturing, and support at your struggle without denying it or pushing it away. They teach you to accept it and love it forward.

Conflict is often selfish. It's all about one person or group getting something at the expense of others. If we all took a step back, we would realize we usually aren't fighting for the common good. Yet, we also usually want what's best for everybody. Survival of the fittest will always tell us to protect ourselves.

Happiness will smother us with promise and hope, and tell us everything is going to be okay.

Sometimes it's hard to understand other people, especially when they are easily irritated.

Like when you keep pronouncing someone's name wrong so they divorce you. So sensitive! Compassion always finds middle ground and soothes differing perspectives.

If you are hard on others, you are hard on yourself

Are you hard on yourself? Would you treat a stranger as poorly as you treat yourself?

Being warm and inviting draws people to you. If you demolished people with anger every time they didn't perform to your expectations, they would never be your friend. Yet, often you may treat yourself with this kind of disregard.

You are relating to yourself twenty-four hours a day. But compassion encourages you to examine what that relationship is like.

Ambitious people are usually hard on themselves. You have an inner urge to improve your life. When you miss a target, doubt and fear scolds you to toughen up and work harder. You may have labeled yourself with some very unforgiving terms. Unless you're the best, you're a complete failure.

Think about someone you really like. Do the words *hardworking, driven, hustler,* or *impatient* come to mind? No. More likely words like *kind, friendly,* or *nice* flavor them. We have to turn this language toward ourselves.

Self-compassion is a feel-good emotion that will help you when times are tough. It moves your momentum from negative to positive by uncomplicating stress. It also creates a sense of safety and security. You need to be, to yourself, the loving, kind friend who always tells you things will be okay. If stress knows you are safe, it will leave you alone. Its job is done. Compassion reaches in and relaxes conditions that complicate your joy.

Your insides being kind to your insides

Self-compassion is relating to yourself kindly. Flaws and all. Compassion for yourself disarms that ancient stress response to fight, flee, or freeze. It soothes you with inner kindness. It is your insides being kind to your insides instead of turning on yourself. You need to routinely create a safe inner world so you're not constantly tricked into fighting for your survival.

Life can be a struggle; it's normal. You need to be understanding of yourself as you experience struggle. It's not your fault. Don't be harsh or judge yourself. Grow toward challenges with compassion as your guide. Compassion and kindness are always in your back pocket to help you feel better and move forward. When everyone else is wrapped up in conflict, you can glide through the complexity.

Here's an example: I was a keynote speaker at a conference of one thousand delegates. In my talk, I was promoting good vibes and happy feelings. At one point someone stood up, called me out, and said, "You're not getting it. Our job is hard. Our industry has taken a serious beating. All this feel-good stuff is just unrealistic. It's not practical."

I hear this kind of thing a lot.

If it had been appropriate, I would have walked over and given that guy a hug, but I sensed he might file a restraining order. It's just that if he gave compassion a chance, something inside him would thaw. I guarantee it. He would open himself up to so much potential. The painful perspective he holds tightly is activating inside him an energy that's really holding him back.

He may have been right, though. Happiness is not practical. Because it's a feeling, not a goal. You don't conquer it, you have it. I wanted him to see that happiness is a lot easier than holding tightly to stress and conflicting opinions.

To encourage an audience like this, I often do a simple activity. I encourage them to start talking about what they appreciate about their work. If I can get an audience shouting out things they love about their job, it flips the momentum and gives people a solid sense of what it's like to feel good about their work. This feel-good vibe can propel entire industries forward.

However, if the predominant vibe is negative, flipping the switch is not so simple. That's okay. I understand. Because the relief for this crowd is compassion. The thing about stress is it causes you to separate from others, become more selfish, and protect yourself; the thing about compassion is it brings people together and creates relief and understanding. Kindness allows you some wiggle room so you can see differing perspectives and learn from them.

Not pretending

Positive thinking gets a bad rap when people think it means ignoring reality and pretending to be happy. That's not what I'm encouraging. Pretending is an act. Happiness is something you let happen. It's a way of being, not an act of doing.

Compassion never pretends things are okay when they're not. You're not slapping lipstick on a problem and labeling it as favorable. Instead, you're melting the stress surrounding your experience and uncomplicating your perspective. The difference is subtle, yet it can be a grand leap into a much more forgiving experience when life hassles you.

Through compassion, you are not changing your experience, you're changing the way you relate to your experience.

Stress compels you to treat every gesture like an item on the list you need to crush. You push ordeals away. Stress keeps people and experiences at arm's length. You create inner resistance to life. Self-kindness shows up as understanding and accepting everything, good or bad. It helps you lift the conditions that keep you from appreciating life.

When you are hard on yourself, you empower stress. Surrounding that feeling with compassion and understanding will tease apart the negative doubts. Fear, worry, doubt, and all stressful emotions are inside you, a part of you. By fighting them, you fight yourself.

Pour some steady love on your fears and doubts, and they give up their grip.

AFFIRMATIONS FOR SELF-LOVE

I give everyone the benefit of the doubt.
I believe in myself.
I know my worth.
When things don't go my way, it's not my fault.
It's normal for me to struggle in challenging situations.
Everything will be okay.
I love myself.
I matter.
I let go of negative thoughts about myself.
I celebrate all my good qualities.
I choose success, health, and happiness.
I experience love wherever I go.
I love myself more every day.

Pour some steady love on your fears and doubts, **and they release their grip.**

Compassion, the game changer

Self-compassion will remodel the insides of you hard-working, driven people. For the better.

Your work ethic has taught you to be tough on yourself. Hidden beneath it is an insecurity that you don't measure up; it propels you to berate yourself as a way of staying motivated. Your goals are a constant reminder that you have more work to do.

As long as any part of you believes you're not good enough, you will always have to try harder. Just to get by. The more you jab yourself with inner criticism, the more motivated you are to keep the self-degrading banter flowing. Your stress cycle loves this as it pours adrenaline into your system and keeps you on high alert. Stress fires up in uncertainty and uses that feeling to prolong the friction.

Stress blankets you with its medieval fury when anything threatens you. It's a complicated feeling that is there to protect you. If you yell at yourself and toughen up against stress, it will put it on alert and feelings of inadequacy will grow stronger.

That is, until self-compassion comes along and disarms stress, coating your whole system with a sense of security, safety, and comfort. How sneaky! It instantly takes you off alert, assuaging your stress. You're no longer on the ledge, toying with survival. This warm, loving mother wraps her arms around you and assures you of safety and security. Circumstances in life can poke at you and try to make you feel bad, but they have to get through Mother first. And she'll kill them with kindness.

Through self-compassion, you become the nourishing mother you wish you had. You're the one who surrounds your insides with a sense of security and safety in the face of fear. Since you put that assurance there, only you can take it away. You can build up a strong inner wall of knowing, safety, confidence, and certainty with compassion that no amount of stress can penetrate. Nothing outside you can tear into this contentment because it is grounded in safety and security. As long as you feel safe, stress doesn't stand a chance.

This sense of security is not conditional. It loves and soothes you no matter what. You don't have to perform to earn its love. Thus it has staying power and isn't hinged on results, circumstances, or approval.

If you could just start labeling your life with compassion, self-love, kindness, and forgiveness, you could transform yourself.

AFFIRMATIONS FOR KINDNESS

I view everyone as good.
I give people the benefit of the doubt.
I see strangers as my friends.
There are good people all around me.
I enjoy being kind to others.
I focus on the good in others.
My thoughts toward others reflect how I feel about myself.
I am surrounded by people who love me.
I listen with compassion to others.
Every person around me enriches my life.
I am loved by others.
I create harmony in relationships.

A kindness practice

I used to be one tough hustler. Secretly, I thought kindness was a very touchy-feely waste of time. I was busy crushing goals. I didn't have time for warm and fuzzy thoughts. But then, as I barreled through my days, I realized something was missing. Following my ambitious trajectory through my career, I spent most of my time fixing deficiencies and proving my worth. Eventually, I noticed joy was missing.

For me, self-kindness emerged within a month, after I steadily spent twenty minutes a day coddling my thoughts and feelings with kindness. I would intentionally stir up thoughts about my value and worth. Soon, a psychological goodwill flourished within me. I blissed out on it often.

I began to notice a tender voice that would comfort me when I felt bad. When I messed up, self-kindness would hint at my value and worth. It swelled inside me and showed understanding for my pain.

This twenty-minute practice took the form of a guided loving kindness meditation. The beautiful yet anonymous lady on my phone told me I have value and to believe in my self-worth. She told me to love myself no matter what. I would continually think kind thoughts and bliss out and sustain the good feelings of compassion. Pretty soon, it naturally flourishes.

For you, I've created a loving kindness meditation on my YouTube channel under the playlist "Bliss Out" (hint: google "Jody Urquhart YouTube Channel" and you'll find me). Check it out and do it as often as you like.

Compassionate day

Hey, hustler—I'd love for you to spend a day haplessly throwing compassion around everywhere. Feel understanding and supportive of everyone for an entire day. Give everyone the benefit of the doubt. Look for ways to relate to their hardship, circumstances, or stress.

Uncomplicate any stressful situation with compassion. Every glaring problem will soften as you understand and relate to it with kindness.

Walk into work and cast compassionate thoughts at the receptionist. Take a call from a client seething with anger and imagine tackling them with a massive hug. Get cut off in traffic and send the impatient drivers tender thoughts of appreciation and love.

Constantly sooth your insides with understanding. Every time you take a breath and sooth stress with compassion, you contact your potential. These good, flowing feelings move you forward by creating acceptance and understanding.

Some people are addicted to the illusion of control that being hard on themselves gives. They think they need the criticism to stay motivated. That being hard on yourself drives performance. Love and compassion, however, are boundless and not attached to expectations. You don't have to perform to be loved. True love will always be in your corner. It never leaves you. It is not pegged to outcomes, and it never judges you. It loves you no matter what.

Pain cracks you open, and most people don't know how to fall apart. Pain is not the inner albatross, but your interpretation of it is. Soften to your insecurities, appreciate your pain, and surround it with love.

The human stress response hasn't evolved much in thousands of years. Most of the time stress deepens and complicates your struggle. It's linked to survival. Survival of our species is much bigger than you can fix. You can't opt out of stress, and it's not your fault. Don't blame yourself for feeling bad or getting caught up in stress. All you can do is accept stress, love yourself up, and grow your enthusiasm for better feelings.

··· FEEL-GOOD HABITS ···

1   **Assess how you treat yourself.** Take out a sheet of paper. Draw a line down the center of it. On the left-hand side, write, *How I Treat Myself.* On the right-hand side, write, *How I Treat a Friend.* Now think about the last time you made a big mistake. Think about the dialogue that went on in your head. Likely it will range from thoughts like *I can't believe I did that* or *How stupid can I be?* to *It's all my fault.* Note these on the left-hand side of the page.

   Think about a good friend going through a similar rough patch. What would you say to them? Likely statements along the lines of *Everything will be okay, This tough situation is not your fault,* and *Don't be so hard on yourself.* Note these on the right-hand side of the page.

   Now compare the words on the two sides of the page. You are staring at the relationship you have with yourself. Begin to consciously say to yourself the soothing words you would say to a friend.

2   **Start your day with kindness to yourself.** Wake up and place your hand on your heart. Breathe in deeply. Say to yourself, "I love you." Take a breath, say it again. Repeat this three times. Do this every day.

3   **Write a kind letter to yourself.** In this letter, direct good wishes toward yourself. Choose phrases like *may I be peaceful, may I be well,* or *may I be happy.* Read it often.

4 **Bliss out on compassion.** Think of an area in your life where you are hard on yourself. Start thinking about yourself in that situation with compassion. Think kind thoughts toward yourself until it starts to feel good. Sustain the good feeling for as long as you can.

5 **Practice sending kind thoughts to others.** Once you've practiced being kind to yourself, it will be easier for you to extend those good wishes to others. Eventually, spread kindness around to people you care about. Once this feels good to you, send kind thoughts to complete strangers. Finally, you will find it rewarding to send compassionate energy to people you have conflict with. Just go lightly at this and reach for feelings of relief from conflict. The smallest amount of relief will hint at tremendous potential. You are broadening your perspective and inviting in happiness and progress. Remember nobody ever has to earn your kind thoughts. Generously flow them to others.

7

FEEL THE ENERGY

YOUR POWERFUL
THOUGHTS VIBRATE

O N A DREARY Sunday afternoon, I sat down next to a Second World War veteran at the B concourse in the Chicago airport. I had time to kill, so I offered to buy him a cocktail. He told me he didn't drink because he was an alcoholic, so I encouraged him to inch closer to the bar so I could enjoy a glass of merlot while we talked.

Over the next hour, he captivated me with war stories. His time in Germany was full of blood, human suffering, and grotesque violence.

He explained that despite everything that happened, he doesn't have any regrets. He said war was a small price to pay for our freedom. With tremendous passion, he explained that our life is so much more precious than we realize. With great certainty, he said that every day we are alive is a profound blessing.

His words magically lifted me. I knew I was meant to meet this optimistic, war-torn veteran.

I looked down at my stilettos and designer purse and wondered if maybe my priorities were messed up. This old gentleman had fought for our freedoms, and all I thought about was properly applied lipstick.

The real beauty of life

The beauty of life is revealed in the invisible emotional currencies of love, gratitude, appreciation, compassion, and joy. These feelings are inside you right now. And your thoughts can guide you in their direction.

Every thought you have has a vibrational quality that either propels you forward with positivity or holds you back in worry or doubt.

Everything you have right now (house, job, spouse, car, dog) started as a thought. If you look at your life and find there are people, circumstances, or situations that you disapprove of, your thoughts and their emotional energy are what make it so. Sure, lousy circumstances happen and can make life difficult, but your repetitive negative thoughts give these circumstances momentum until they appear in your life.

If you own that your current thoughts create your future, you will experience a new sense of power. To amend your future, change your thoughts about it. Uplifting positive thoughts have a vibrational frequency that, if you sustain it, will propel you forward.

Now, I can already hear you saying, *It sounds so simple—it can't possibly be that easy or everyone would do it. Isn't it hard to change your thoughts?*

So, try this:

1 Think about a cat.
2 Now think about a dog.

You just changed your thoughts. Was that hard?

The only thing that makes this hard is clinging to complex negative thoughts. The more often you return to negative thoughts, the more depleting and engrained they become.

Society is predominantly negative because negativity is durable. A negative mindset just gets more and more convoluted and complex. It keeps digging around for more trouble. Positive thoughts and feelings are easy and fleeting. It's not that we'd rather be drained than uplifted, but negativity has complexity and staying power. Positivity doesn't.

When you feel a pang of negative emotions, it means you have been thinking a troubling thought—you may even be returning to it often. By perpetuating it, you are building negative momentum.

You need to find a way to let that thought go. Stop your mind from using you—make it your servant, not your master. If you have negative momentum, repetitive thoughts that hold you in doubt may be wearing you thin. The fear of what could happen is making nothing happen in your life.

Calm and harmony sound perfect, but stress keeps nagging you about your obligations. Send stress on a sabbatical and take over steering your life. How? With your thoughts.

If you can bliss out and sustain a high-vibration thought, you build forward momentum.

Attention spans

Attention spans have dwindled with the deluge of information today. So has the quality of our thoughts. If you are constantly bombarded with negative information, it takes conscious effort to keep a positive focus.

When I go to the grocery store with my three-year-old nephew, I steer clear of the candy aisle. If I don't, he will think of nothing but candy and never stop begging for sweets. But if I skip that aisle, candy won't even come up.

I have a lot of faith in adult human beings; however, our attention spans aren't much better than that of a three-year-old. We're easily distracted. Anything shiny and appealing can pull us in another direction, whether it's good for us or not. Through the media, we are more faithfully drawn to combat and negativity. It would be a lot easier to promote positivity if you could skip over negative rhetoric and stay focused on what you want.

Focus on what you want

Our true power is in corralling our messy thoughts and focusing them on what we want, not obsessing about what we don't like. Our thoughts create a powerful point of attraction that shapes our lives. Leaving them unchecked, they tend to glom on to negativity and problems. It can make a beautiful life messy.

To take control of your life, you need to control your thoughts. Tell your brain what you want. Don't be bashful or complicated. Be unapologetic and bold about how you want to feel and what you want to accomplish.

This doesn't require years of self-reflection. I'll give you a few clues. You likely want health, happiness, energy, success, and so on.

Most people want the same things, and most people don't have them because the narratives we incessantly entertain provoke fear. Most people spend more time thinking about what they don't want instead of what they do.

The control panel to your life is your brain. Your thoughts. You must be relentless about keeping your attention on the things you want. If you want health, talk to yourself about your health. Instead of regurgitating thoughts about your bad back or weak ankles, invite in strength and stamina. The inner banter about your bellyache alerts stress, saying you have a problem. Stress responds by tightening muscles in your stomach, provoking more pain. Take control. Invite calm and relaxation to inhabit the lining of your stomach. Spurred by your thoughts, gentle guidance will dissolve tension and give you some breathing room.

You can't control thoughts happening, but **you can decide not to be carried away by them.**

If you want financial freedom, then free yourself from thoughts of scarcity. Ask for wealth instead of besieging your mind with ideas about being broke. Your life doesn't have to revolve around a line of credit. Think about prosperity.

It takes persistence to change the narrative. Keep telling yourself what you want, not what you don't want. Keep labeling life in a positive way.

Pepper your brain with sound bites of prosperity and hope. Bliss out on those feelings when you can. The world around you wants to tell you that conflict is news, but you know better. Your story is about thriving.

A word about money

A lot of people are interested in attracting wealth and prosperity.

This is a nice focus because feelings of success make you feel good. However, I recommend you concentrate on broader happiness as a launching point. That's an easier vibe to tap into, and it's not attached to an outcome. It's less complicated.

Once you find your happy place more often, your whole life moves in a good direction. Through this positive momentum you can easily get whatever you want. Anything you ask for comes quite naturally. You see opportunities not obstacles on your way to prosperity. Thoughts of appreciation, gratitude, and love are good-vibe generators that gain momentum and make everything else easier. A new car, a beautiful house, more money, great relationships—all these are the byproducts of good feelings.

Remember you are after the joy in the journey, not the outcomes. Just get your direction right and don't worry about the destination.

AFFIRMATIONS FOR PROSPERITY

I deserve success.
I attract abundance.
I consistently find opportunities.
I happily accept money.
I am worth what I charge.
I always have enough money.
I make money easily.
I use money to help others.
Money is a frequency.
I use my unique talents to attract wealth.
Every dream I have is coming true.
I am a magnet for money.

Rewrite your story

At an event a few years ago, I was introduced to a speaker. He told me his speech was about how he was badly beaten up at five years old. I blurted out, "Wow, that was a long time ago!" The man standing in front of me looked to be over sixty.

He said, "Yes. Being a victim of violence is terrible. It's a life-altering experience."

Definitely! But when do we get to let go of our past? I wanted to embrace the man and say, *I know it was hard on you, but you have to move on.*

I don't mean to be insensitive. My point is that this same man has won awards for his research. Why not tell that story instead?

The story you tell about yourself the most becomes who you are, because you keep it alive by telling it.

What's your story? Is it a bad experience you survived? If it is, focus on the survival part. Tell people about your strengths, or your ability to see the good in the bad. Don't let a tragic past experience be your present. Life is waiting.

In fact, you could make this an exercise to increase your awareness of your predominant thoughts. What story about yourself do you tell the most? Do you focus on hope and optimism or fear and challenge? Rewrite your story by labeling the positive lessons.

It might also help you to write down some of your thoughts during the day. Stay neutral and don't judge yourself. Randomly write down your thoughts. Beside the thought, write how it made you feel.

That's it. Analyzing the thoughts will not help you. It will only complicate matters. We always want to move positively forward into the future, and no amount of analyzing the past will do that.

Thought reels

Do you talk to yourself? I do. A lot. Inside my head is a constant stream of thoughts. They have no apparent direction, unless I guide them.

Often I am triggered by my environment, and my head floods with somber and contagious thoughts. I tend to chase the thoughts that terrorize me the most. Draining thoughts can run on a loop in my head for as long as I keep entertaining them.

I'm not alone. Most people have a thinking problem.

Endless reels of torturous thoughts harass us daily. Your mind produces an impressive amount of thoughts that paint the world as a scene akin to the hit reality TV show *Survivor*. You are seduced by stress. Even tiny stresses seem to have devastating urgency.

Changing your predominant thoughts will set you free.

Studies have shown we have anywhere from twelve thousand to sixty thousand thoughts daily. An article published by the National Science Foundation indicated that 80 percent of them are negative and around 95 percent are the same thoughts we had the day before.[6]

We don't tend to get lost in thoughts of gratitude and love. Instead, we're gripped by thoughts of anger and animosity. Joyful, pleasurable thoughts are short-lived, but fear and anguish stick to you like glue. Especially when uncertainty looms in any pocket of your world.

You can thank your stress response for that. Negative thoughts are enticing because they perpetuate the stress cycle. Provoked by thoughts, the emotional brain takes over, and you become easily triggered. When they circle around in your head, they drown you in adrenaline and put you on high alert. They continue to make you worry and prepare you for the worst. Evolutionarily, this helped humans survive, and it's why negative thoughts are so gritty and tenacious.

Positive thoughts are lovely. They release dopamine, oxytocin, and serotonin. These feel-good hormones have the opposite effect of adrenaline and cortisol (stress hormones). They relax you. They disengage the stress cycle and quiet the emotional brain. The prefrontal cortex takes over, and you become calmer and focused.

Obviously positive thoughts are better for your health, and the good news is the brain can change. It's constantly organizing itself. It forms new connections between neurons whenever something is learned. We can teach our brain to be positive just by introducing more positive thoughts.

The fear of what could happen is **making nothing happen in your life.**

How to stop negative thoughts

You may have been told to stop being negative; it seems difficult because you can't stop your thoughts. They erupt spontaneously in your brain, and you can't just tell them to stop and they'll go away. We are always thinking.

The idea isn't to banish negative thoughts. Instead, be curious about them. Just don't chase them around and hold onto them for so long.

Here's an example. Your frenemy at work keeps maneuvering to make you look bad. She miscommunicated a deadline. She stole a project. She's after the promotion you want. Thinking about all this is complicated and draining. Yet you can't seem to let the thoughts go. They keep getting more convoluted (*She's like an evil stepsister*; *How could she smile at me like that with the knife behind her back?*; *She's clearly out to destroy me*). And you keep feeling worse.

You have options to change this negative thought momentum.

You could release the thoughts sooner. The longer you focus on any negative thought, the more activated, polluted, and complex it becomes.

You could purposely not return to any negative thought. Because negativity is complex, you will never be able to sort it out, so you will want to keep trying. The more you try, the more complicated it will get.

You could lift the conditions that cause the negative momentum. The condition is your frenemy needs to act appropriately for you to be happy. You let this go by realizing you have no control over her behavior, by gradually looking for the good in her, and by forgiving her. Slowly assign more positive labels to your frenemy.

In a short time, through massaging your labels, she can go from evil to appreciated in a sequence that looks a bit like this:

I think this woman is ... evil → confused → having a difficult time → in need of support → totally relatable in her pain → a friend who I appreciate → someone I admire

By directing your thoughts and labels, you guide your negative emotions in a positive direction. You move your momentum from negative to positive.

Trying to lasso your wild thoughts and wrestle them to the ground will only fuel their fury.

Slowly cut off the oxygen supply to the thoughts and lingering emotions that bring you down.

Just be aware of when your thoughts are headed in a negative direction and let those thoughts go if you can, or massage them into more positive territory. Always move your thoughts in the direction of what you want (happiness, success, love, progress, and so on) instead of what you don't want (conflict, stress, confusion ...).

A routine of happiness

We've already touched on so many happiness practices. Visualization, affirmation, gratitude, appreciation, focus on strengths, believe in others, positive labeling ... Pick up any one of these techniques often to help you feel good. Do not attach these feelings to any specific outcome. Just dream and believe.

Start as soon as you wake up, and imagine a great day unfolding. Everything is working out for you, and you feel wonderful. You feel content, joyful, and uplifted. Think of events coming up in your day, like planned meetings, and imagine handling them with grace and ease. People are smiling, and everyone is happy.

Label all parts of your job and all people in it as *kind, happy,* and *a reward to work with.*

Bliss out and feel amazing in this visualization. You want to build a reservoir of positive energy. If you can continue throughout your day with positive affirmations reeling around in your head and feel good about the words, you will gain a distinct positive momentum. Actively lift the energy vibration of your day simply by thinking and feeling positive. Sustain these uplifting feelings for a while.

Now what if your day disappoints and contrasts your happy vision? What if people aren't smiling and happy but are angry and distressed? Don't they know they're supposed to be happy?

This is a wonderful opportunity for you. Because you have built up the positive momentum through your thoughts, they can't stomp out your good vibes. Keep flowing positive labels to your colleagues.

Think of yourself as a buoyant energy teasing apart tension at work. Comfort stress with compassion. Skim over conflict and keep your happy vibes.

Use any excuse to feel good and see what happens.

Take this lightly; happiness is easy, after all.

AFFIRMATIONS FOR GRATITUDE

I am grateful for everything I have.
Every day is a blessing.
I am happy and grateful.
I celebrate life every day.
I think positive thoughts easily.
Being positive is easy for me.
I see opportunities in stressful situations.
I am successful.
Today I am happy.
My challenges help me grow.
I am capable of so much.
I love my job, and I love my co-workers.
Today is going to be an awesome day.
I can do anything I put my mind to.
I can get through anything.
Every day, I am more grateful for what I have.
I am thankful for my life.

· · · FEEL-GOOD HABITS · · ·

1 **Allow yourself to complain about something three times only.** After complaining three times, do not chase that thought anymore. You will need to be diligent and climb out of the complaint every time. Think about and feel something positive instead.

2 **Let go of negative thoughts sooner.** When you are caught in a negative thought, don't let it spiral out of control. Let go of the complexity of the thought and refocus. Ask yourself what you want—get your direction right.

3 **Check in on your positive affirmation routine.** Have affirmations become routine yet? Commit to keeping positive, uplifting emotions inside you. In any downtime, like driving or waiting for an elevator, pepper your brain with positive thoughts. Bring an affirmation to mind and let the feeling expand into your body.

4 **Be positive in the morning and evening.** First thing in the morning and last thing before you go to bed, your brain is most susceptible. I recommend journaling at these times. Write about what you're grateful for, recalling all the good things that happened in your life. Or you may want to repeat positive affirmations. Alternatively you can visualize things going well, achieving goals, and having fun along the way.

Check out my motivational speeches on YouTube (under the "Bliss Out" playlist) specifically for this. Play them before bed and first thing in the morning.

8

MOVE YOUR RELATIONSHIPS FORWARD

BELIEVE IN OTHERS— DON'T WORRY ABOUT THEM

MY DAD has the newspaper delivered to his doorstep every morning. For more than fifty years he's relied on this print edition to start his day and make sure he knows what's happening in the world.

One day, when his faithful paper didn't appear on the doorstep, I explained to him that he could always read the online version of the newspaper.

I told him that when you read the print version, it's old news. By the time they write the story, print it, and deliver it to your doorstep, things have changed. He would need to go to the online version to see important updates about what's going on in our world. However, my dad remains content with viewing yesterday's news as if it were today's.

Most of us live our lives based on yesterday's news. It's the print version, not the live one. Everything in your life right now is yesterday's, last week's, or last year's news: You bought the house you live in years ago; you've been in your job for a while; your relationship has stood the test of time. Everything you have is a result of thoughts and actions that have created your current reality. Unless you are continually bringing a curious, fresh perspective to your current situation, you may start to feel stuck.

Recognize the great love, opportunity, and beauty in the life you have right now. When you've had something in your life for a while, you tend to take it for granted and lose a sense of its value. After all, yesterday's news isn't so new anymore. Get into the habit of appreciating life—not tolerating it.

If your life feels stuck, you're likely too heavily focused on problems. Troubled circumstances are springing forward from the past. Yesterday's news is gnawing at you to move forward, but your focus on problems glues you to your past.

If you get into the habit of looking at old news and repeated challenges from an uplifting, expansive perspective, you can reinvent your life from the inside out. You will start to move forward. The curiosity and passion you bring to your life will broaden your perspective and hint toward potential.

But this often gets most complicated in how we relate to others. We keep trying to hold people to their past, when what we all want is to appreciate others and believe in them.

Focus on the good news

Just like feeling good, relationships can be easy. If they are not, we are complicating them with our perspective. Any relationship that feels bad for you has negative momentum. This means you are consistently going into the past, yesterday's news, and regurgitating fear, worry, and doubt about the relationship or person. This holds you both back.

Wouldn't you rather update your newsfeed with examples of how you are both moving forward? Wouldn't you rather be inspired and believe in others?

Recently, I was standing in line at the grocery store. The woman behind me ran into a dear old friend, and they started catching each other up on their lives. I was eavesdropping.

What we all want is to enjoy the present and create a beautiful future.

One of the pair gave the other a detailed description of her two sons—the good son and the bad son. The good son's life was terrific, being the smart, accomplished architect that he is. He had been working on creating a great community in lower east villages. He has an amazing wife and two adorable kids. Everything was so rosy.

The picture of the bad son, however, looked quite different. He was troubled. In a sorry state, he lost his job and now has to keep borrowing money. He just got divorced and has a strained relationship with his kids. He just couldn't catch a break or get ahead. She painted him as the poster child for a troubled life.

I think most parents mean well. I could hear in her voice that this mom had huge love in her heart for both her sons. But she was not helping her "bad son." She gave him the unforgiving label—*bad*. All those conditions she placed on her bad son, to be like his brother, had to be stifling him and their relationship. Love can't find any breathing room between two people when these kinds of rules are placed on it.

What could this mom do to help her bad son?

Could she lift the conditions she placed on him? She would need to stop trying to fix him. He's not broken, and he's not his brother. If she could steadily think high-vibration thoughts of unconditional love, compassion, and appreciation for him, it would move their relationship forward. Instead of worrying about him, she could label his strengths and focus on those, without giving him advice about how to improve. Every time she starts frisking his life for problems and suggesting improvements, she likely makes him feel bad. If she stopped talking about the old news, problems, and regrets of the past and guided him to feel good by appreciating when things went well for him, that would be a fabulous start.

Whenever they had fun and felt good together, or when she gleaned that he felt good about anything, she would know the positivity was working. He would be moving forward. Soon, their relationship would start to take shape in a positive way.

This is a simple mental habit. Instead of worrying about her son, she could believe in him. Instead of looking at his past to point out problems, she could look to his future for potential. It's a fresh, expansive, updated perspective of his life.

Every time she thinks and feels good about her son, she is lifting the energy vibration of her relationship with her son. The more she goes back to these good-vibe-producing thoughts, the more activated they become and the more their relationship springs forward in a positive direction.

Seductive negativity

Some negative topics between people are so compelling that they draw you back, again and again, to complain about a nasty boss, filthy neighbor, or the wayward government.

When these topics become the point of attraction in your relationship (as a couple or a group), you talk about them a lot. Let's say you regularly gripe about how bad your job is with certain colleagues around the water cooler. Soon, these draining assessments you share about your job become what powerfully attracts you to these colleagues. The topic of your conversation will always wind its way back to these hard thoughts and feelings about your work circumstances.

Every time you return to them and think about them, they get stronger. Some topics are so energized that the chemical cocktail they instantaneously produce in your body is toxic. It's like a hangover because you keep indulging in these topics and they make you feel worse. Imagine this happening to a group of people all at once!

Stay away from those topics as much as possible! Find fun things to discuss. Very shortly, because you're not paying attention to those negative thoughts, they will lose their grip. Your relationships will improve, as will your moods, and the beautiful thing is, you don't have to do anything at all—you've actually just stopped complaining. You changed your thoughts to a higher-quality blissed-out vibration that will change your momentum.

Dealing with strained relationships

Seek out ways to feel better about any strained relationships you're in. You need to clear up the worry, doubt, or any old news with a positive perspective. If possible, don't limp around in the past or talk about problems.

Some relationships are conditioned to be negative and to constantly regurgitate the past. If your conversation does go down a path besmirched with problems, try to reframe the topics in a positive way. You might say or think something as simple as, *Oh well, I guess he was just doing the best he can.*

To clean up negative momentum in your mind, playfully poke at any conditions you are placing on happiness, love, or joy with this person. Focus on positive aspects of your relationship and stay away from complaining, worrying, or recapitulating problems.

Also know that you do not need anyone to change for you to feel good. If you start thinking positively, but others keep launching negativity and doubt at you, keep refocusing on your own good feelings and path. You don't need them to change. That would just place more conditions on your own joy. You also might consider taking a break from relationships held together by negativity. You're not helping each other.

AFFIRMATIONS FOR FORGIVENESS AND FEELING GOOD

I forgive my past.
I forgive myself for anger, worry, and doubt.
I don't need to be perfect to be happy.
I forgive myself for my mistakes.
I forgive others.
For me to feel good, I don't need others to feel good.
I feel good, and I don't need anyone's approval.

Stop trying to fix people

I know you mean well, but trying to fix people usually doesn't work out well. For instance, telling someone they need to get a job so their life will improve will likely backfire. That kind of statement conveys a condition. For them to be happy (or for you to be happy), they need to get a job. I've met many unemployed people who are happy. Instead of manipulating and trying to fix people's lives, help them feel good. Believe in them.

Any of the following statements would be an improvement on *you need to get a job*:

- It's such a worthwhile feeling to be a part of something bigger.

- It's so rewarding learning new skills and meeting new people every day.

- You have so much to offer.

- There are so many organizations that would benefit from your skill and enthusiasm.

Appreciate life,
don't tolerate it.

- It feels so good to get up in the morning with somewhere meaningful to go.

- It's great to feel like a part of a group that cares about what you do.

These statements remind someone of what it feels like to have a good job. This may inspire them to get one. Anytime you zoom in on fixing something or someone, you are making them into a problem. If you lift this mindset, you will discover there is no problem. These are simply nuances guiding you toward more understanding and potential.

Rather than trying to fix people, highlight the positive, guide people toward their strengths, express gratitude for your relationship, or show them unconditional love. Gradually your relationship will move forward, and so will they.

Let's consider Mary, who hates her job and constantly complains about it. To help a friend like this, guide her perspective in a positive direction. When Mary wants to complain, show her compassion and empathy with responses like "That must have been hard" or "That sounds challenging." Resist the temptation to egg her on in tearing apart her job. Instead, look for small opportunities to nudge her in a positive direction:

- You could remind her of how her job has helped her grow.

- You could point out positive aspects of the work.

- You could highlight her strengths.

- You could show her how she's impacting customers or contributing to the team.

- You could ask her about the reasons she took the job (they will be positive or she wouldn't have taken it).

None of this should be a veiled attempt to fix Mary. She's not broken. She just needs to remember what it's like to feel good about her work.

Most importantly, edge Mary toward her positive feelings with statements like "It must have felt great to..." or "You sound so proud of..." or "What a relief to..." Likewise, "You sound so happy with..." or "I love your enthusiasm..." or "Your passion is clear."

Help people put positive energy inside themselves by talking about their positive feelings. Getting wind of a higher vibration can change a point of attraction. People naturally start to focus on what they really want.

• • • FEEL-GOOD HABITS • • •

1   **Clear negative momentum.** In any relationship that is strained in your life, clear up negative momentum. Release any negative conditions and labels (see the exercises in Chapter 1). Avoid negative topics or subjects you both tend to be drawn to. Use compassion and kindness anytime you feel bad about them. Give them the benefit of the doubt. Use a more positive label that feels better (for instance, *parts of my job are rewarding, I learn new things every day, I love working with my colleagues,* or *my customers are great*). Return to these positive thoughts often.

2   **Help others.** Think of anyone who is struggling that you long to help. Release any thoughts of worry for them and instead believe in their strengths. Look for statements to help them feel better about their situation:

   • This would be hard for anyone, you do handle this well.
   • You sound hopeful about . . .
   • Your thoughts about this are so inspiring.
   • Your perspective on this is so hopeful.
   • I love your optimism about . . .
   • You're such a positive person.
   • You're so good at . . .
   • What would you like to see happen?

3   **Clear up worry.** When you worry about someone, write down all your worries on a piece of paper: *My son may never*

get a job. My spouse isn't taking care of himself. My brother is always sick. Lift any conditions these worries suggest (that your son needs a job, your spouse needs to take care of himself, your brother needs to stop complaining about his health) by not focusing on them. Then put positive labels on them: *My son is smart and capable. My spouse knows how to take care of himself. My brother is doing well—he looks happy.* Every time you want to worry, nudge at it with some kindness and return to the positive label.

4 **Spread love.** Anytime you have pent up bad feelings about someone, try spreading invisible love and kindness all over them. Don't tell them about your secret affectionate thoughts. None of this is tied to a goal or urging any sort of outcome. Just radiate thoughts and feelings of love toward them. Bliss out on these good feelings. Wish them well and wish them happiness. Do this three times a day for a minute at a time and your relationship will evolve. Note that the perpetrator of your bad feelings doesn't change at all, but you do. You are removing your aversion to this person and opening the relationship up to possibility. They will start to look different to you. You have built up compassion around them.

5 **Put yourself in their shoes.** In any challenging situation with a difficult person, imagine their side of the story. Try to stay neutral and appreciate where they are coming from. Instead of labeling them as a problem, see their potential.

9

BE AN INSPIRING LEADER

JOY IS AN INSIDE JOB

NOW THAT you understand the incredible power of your thoughts and feelings, leading others will be a joy.

The best leaders lead with passion, optimism, care, and belief in others. These uplifting, buoyant thoughts and feelings draw out enthusiasm, and the good feelings build positive momentum. Teams move forward.

Truly inspired leadership is rare because most leaders look at performance and outcomes and demand results. When they don't see their team producing results, they try to control them.

Trying to control others is always depleting. Inspiring others is about building uplifting thoughts, energy, and feelings, and achieving goals.

If you're a leader and your team is struggling with poor morale, this could be why: your direction is mixed up. You manipulate others so you can be happy with their performance. But joy is an inside job. Conditions of control will squeeze joy out of your relationships. Lift the conditions and put your faith in inspiration.

To inspire others you have to be inspired. Your leadership has to come from a powerful, uplifting place of hope, enthusiasm, passion, prosperity, purpose, appreciation, love, or joy. The way you lead yourself is the same way you lead others. If you're not kind to yourself, you can't be kind to others. Focus on feeling good first and then use that feeling to lead your team forward and build positive momentum.

Results are past tense

The results you keep focusing on are past tense. If you can see them, they've already happened. You want your team to get ahead of results with high-vibing emotional velocity thoughts that spur excellent work. Results are the aftermath.

Results are valuable information to give direction and insight. A leader's job is to steer momentum in a positive direction through engaged, happy employees and a focus on the future. In the coming pages, I give you inspired leadership examples. I encourage you to notice how, in each instance, the leader focuses on uplifting thoughts and feelings instead of trying to control people.

Let's say you want your team members to care more about customer service. You can set policy and bark orders when they don't comply. This is sure to cause resentment. You and your team, even your customers, may develop bad feelings toward you.

If you approach service as a problem to fix, it will always be a problem because this is your focus (or label). A better way is to start with what you want first. That's probably a team that thrives in taking care of customers. So, focus on that. How do you want people to think and feel about customer service? Likely you want your team to care about their customers and build long-term relationships with them. So, introduce a label to them as a *dedicated, caring team*. Imagine your team zipping around, purposefully engaged in servicing customers. This team deeply cares about helping out. They love their customers and really want to make their day.

Notice these are all simple, light, buoyant thoughts. They are easy, they should feel good. Problems are complicated, your goals or policies may be complicated, but feeling good isn't.

Also notice that now you are solutions oriented instead of problem focused. A big deal in shaping morale is setting intentions and honoring feelings. Keep people thinking about moving forward toward solutions, instead of being bogged down with past poor outcomes.

It's simple. You want people to move forward and feel good at work. You want them to feel good about their jobs. Good about their customers.

Help people move forward

Keep the team focused on the future not the past. They all came to their jobs to progress in their lives, so help them do that. Focus on solutions driving the future instead of problems hooking them to the past. This naturally means you focus less on what went wrong (problems) and more on what goes right (solutions). This is your momentum. It's powerful.

Celebrate success, opportunities, and helpful solutions. As a leader, keep a pulse on this forward momentum. If the work has a sinking or waning quality, you know people are too focused on problems. They are stuck because they keep regurgitating what went wrong in the past.

Problems are the past, solutions are the future. Think of problems as information coming forward from past efforts to give you guidance. They are an opportunity to adjust your course. They are not meant to stall your team. Solutions propel you forward. They offer a vision of how you want things to happen, how you want people to feel. Solutions create something new and exciting for teams and clients to look forward to. If possible, lift any label your team has that causes them to view anything on the job as a problem. Label things positively so your team is inclined to keep seeing potential and moving forward.

To inspire others,
**you have to
be inspired.**

Help people feel good

Helping people feel good doesn't mean you are responsible for how they feel. It does, however, suggest that you inspire good feelings in them. The thought vibration is different. Needing people to be happy or inspired creates attachment to the way they feel—that is draining. Being inspired and believing in others feels good.

Grant was worried about his employee, Sarah, who wasn't learning the skills required to do her new job. This was becoming a problem as he kept returning to depleting thoughts of worry and doubt about her abilities. He knew that, as a leader, he needed to inspire her, but he didn't know how.

It would be difficult for Grant to inspire his employees if he was not inspired himself. Worry and doubt about others are not inspiring feelings. But if Grant were to shift perspective so that he could inspire his team, if he were to believe in Sarah, highlight her strengths, and be hopeful about her future, his uplifting perspective would move them both forward. Sarah would no longer be a problem; instead, her strengths would constantly be revealed.

It's a simple but profound feel-good habit. Lead with solutions, opportunities, strengths, and potential. Believe in others, don't worry about them.

Lead with optimism

Start by sharing with others what you feel good about at your work. Is it positive relationships? Progress? Team success? Share with them an uplifting vision of the future. Point out positive aspects of the job, the customers, your team.

A leader's job isn't to manipulate their team's world to make it more pleasing for them. This would be complicated. But can you coax positive emotion out from inside them? When you see someone happy, notice it. Value it, but don't attach it to an external perk. If you want your team to ooze passion from the inside out, focus on thoughts and feelings that provoke passion. You might say, "Team, I love watching your passion come alive on this project. It's clear nothing can stop you because you're so committed to caring for your customers." Keep pointing out positive aspects about the job, the team, your customers, and your industry.

Celebrate cooperative acts. When a team comes together in a caring way to help others, focus on it. Appreciate how good it feels to care for each other.

Keep guiding your team with positive, visionary thoughts about progress and success.

External perks

Many organizations rely on external rewards and perks like bonuses, snacks, employee of the month, extra time off, or coffee gift cards to recognize achievements. If they feel good to people and don't create competition or entitlement, they are great. However they may muddy the waters when it comes to morale.

My son's soccer coach gives all the kids on the team a medal. He says the reasoning behind it is to put hard work and effort on the pedestal, not results. Winning isn't as important as trying. The life lesson is that as long as you work hard, you'll get ahead. In reality, some of the kids don't try because winning doesn't matter; they'll still get a medal. And you don't need a medal to feel happy or successful. It's the joy of the activity, learning, and being a part of a team that matters. Leadership is a lot easier if you just continually share uplifting visionary thoughts of the future while celebrating progress and good feelings on your team.

When you peg inner happiness on outward perks, awards, and medals, it often messes everything up. People who are constantly rewarded for doing their job will eventually come to feel entitled to external perks instead of just appreciating the job and the value they authentically add to it. External rewards can mess up morale because the real reward for most work is within. Remember that people choose their jobs because they feel good about the opportunity and want to grow. Success is an energizing feeling inside that makes people feel good to be a part of something. Medals and perks can trivialize those good feelings and teach people to demand something in return for their effort.

For most leaders their team's success is a concrete goal, but it's also a powerful feeling. Teams may be tempted to skip the journey and go directly to success so they can achieve a reward. It's quicker. But they miss out on good feelings that will expand past the reward and grow into further potential. Also, the destination is nowhere near as enticing as the journey.

For instance, Jason is a leader who longs for an inspired team; but more importantly, he wants results. He constantly pushes his team to reach their goals and offers them accolades and rewards when they do. However, turnover is high, and people are burnt out.

Jason and his team are laser-focused on their goals. It's an environment that demands success. But the team's focus is not on success, it's on the demands leading up to success. They are focused on a lack of success and the problems that get in the way of progress.

They cut out the joy of the job in favor of results. Have a look:

- Instead of providing value to others, Jason's team stresses over results.

- Instead of enjoying serving customers, Jason's team responds to complaints.

- Instead of appreciating success, Jason's team feels pressure to conquer the next goal.

If Jason could focus on the forward positive direction of the team, celebrate even small wins, instead of the final goal or destination, he would generate the success the team wants instead of the problems preventing it. Through this expansive outlook his team would appreciate more joy in their job and see more opportunities to serve others. The feelings of success would flourish and so would his team. Goals are still a priority, and they are the product of the work. They guide you, but they are not the journey. The joy is the journey.

Consider these statements and their focus on people feeling good and moving forward:

- Carlos, your love for your customers is palpable. I noticed your remarkable delight today processing orders. It's like you can imagine the delight in your customers' eyes with every order you touch.

- Jacquie, you have a spring in your step. It's magical watching you at work today. I can tell you're really loving this project.

- Kevin, it's obvious the joy you have for this work. We're so glad to have you as a part of this team.

- Han, I can tell you thrive on this team. Your optimism and enthusiasm are contagious.

- Farhan, you are always smiling and clearly having a great time. Watching you have so much fun at work is rewarding for everyone.

- Lee, your compassion for your patients is undeniable. I'm honored to watch you help them heal with dignity and love.

Aim to inspire good feelings in others **instead of trying to change them.**

- Amanda, you are such a cheerful person, and I so appreciate how you continuously look for the best in others.

- Team, this morning started out rough. It's hard to take the criticism we did. I was so proud to witness the turnaround as you all clung to hope and passion. You leaned on each other, you cared for each other, and it made us stronger than the criticism. Today we proved that as long as we have each other, we will thrive.

Notice how these statements celebrate feelings rather than outcomes, which taps into an inner drive. When your intention is inspiring others, avoid platitudes like *keep up the good work*.

Focus on the joy of the journey, not the destination.

Rules versus transparency

Very often, rules are established because we don't trust our people. Something went wrong, and now we have to punish everyone. But rules can be conditions that diminish happiness when they punish people with the past. Instead, find a positive label and let that lead people forward. For instance, if a team member gave unverified information to a customer and you found out, you might instate a rule about restricting information. But what you really want is transparency, so label transparent acts as *good* and move forward.

Flip the problem around, and trust people first. Rules should be guidelines to help people make informed decisions. But lead with trust.

Obviously, you're still going to need goals and job descriptions. But these don't need to be the only engines driving you. Achieving a goal is a by-product of inspired work. The longer you, as the leader, or the team stare at the goal or push it around hoping it will perform, the further away a feeling of success will be. When crushing goals and taking care of the job is fueled by inspiration, everything is easier.

Start by sparking feelings of success. This innate passion moves you forward. Set your goals with intention and excitement about the future instead of fear or worry from the past. Know you are aiming for them because they will help you progress rather than because you're responding to a poor performance.

Always point your team in the direction of where they are going, not where they're at.

When you want your team to reach a goal, talk to them about the passion it will take to get there. Show them that passion that will fuel the progress. Paint them a picture of inspiration, pulling the team together. Inspire a vision that brings the feeling of success to them now, before conquering the goal.

AFFIRMATIONS FOR LEADERSHIP

Our work is inspiring.
My team loves helping others.
My team members really care about one another.
Our work is so meaningful.
Our customers really value us.
My team is more inspired every day.
My team has purpose and passion.
My team is like a family.
We are getting better every day.
We all enjoy our work.

Keep a pulse on morale

As a leader, notice momentum from results and good feelings. If people are positive, great. Keep appreciating that. When you see people progress, celebrate that too. Everyone on your team took the job they have because it looked like an opportunity for them. Now they want to move forward, so recognize when they do. Reinforce team and individual progress. Connect their good feelings with the progress. It also helps when teams can remind customers of progress they have made and continually point them forward toward more solutions.

You must also notice any negative momentum on your team, any delible stuck or negative feeling around someone or something at work. To turn the momentum around, help your team lift the conditions that are making them feel bad.

Consider a situation on Fatima's team. Several of her team members were unhappy with one another. They could be happy, she knew, but most were holding tightly to the condition that others should stop being difficult—as in, stop telling me what to do, stop inundating me with requests. People were so focused on the difficulties that morale was plummeting, and so was engagement.

To reverse this negative momentum, Fatima aimed to help her team feel better about each other and their conflict. She pointed out the positive sides of differing perspectives. She emphasized that requests for collaboration meant respect for a person's ability, that a seemingly bossy co-worker helped the whole team meet deadlines. When one team member rolled her eyes in disgust at that last point, Fatima knew that label didn't feel good. So it wouldn't work.

She began to routinely appreciate each team member's strengths, nudging her team toward neutral and eventually positive momentum. She told her team how much she appreciated it when they valued each other. She reminded them how good it feels to be genuinely recognized by colleagues. She would say things like, "Gerald, I'm thankful for how you see the good in others. Watching you give people the benefit of the doubt is inspiring."

Try something similar with as many employees as you can—and be genuine.

You might create a forum or program that encourages people to recognize others. Just make sure to stay attuned to how it feels for your team. It won't work if the initiative is seen as a way to force compliance with a new appreciation protocol. Trying to make people be positive is like trying to catch a falling knife: a lot depends on which end lands in your hands. If people perceive your programs as a veiled attempt to cover up problems, it will breed resentment. Instead, look for ways to nudge people to feel good about themselves or their jobs by highlighting progress or purpose.

··· FEEL-GOOD HABITS ···

1 **Bliss out on inner inspiration.** Try a feel-good visualization to connect with inspiration at work. Visualizations are best when they are short. So get in, feel good, and get out. Do this anytime you need a quick energy boost:

- Imagine yourself totally inspired by your work.
- Imagine the day flying by because it's so engaging and fun.
- Imagine your team engaged in purposeful, meaningful work.
- Imagine your clients appreciating the work you do.

Hold the feelings of inspiration inside you long enough to sustain that feeling of bliss.

2 **Inspire others with positive labels.** Every day, aim to inspire positive feelings in a couple of team members. In advance, think about what feeling you want to inspire (for example, hope, joy, success, or optimism) and what you will say to bring it out in them. Keep it simple. You could notice someone being enthusiastic and say, "I love your optimism." Just by labeling their behavior positively you are putting their attention on optimism. To inspire hope, talk about something hopeful about the future. Inspire joy by pointing out joyful acts, people, or aspects of the job. Inspire success by calling out and appreciating successful attributes. Revel in and celebrate progress. All that matters is how you and your team feel about your words.

3   **Bliss out on meaningful work.** Every job has meaning. The simple act of focusing on it is very rewarding. When a team starts their day, it's a great time to rally them and bliss out on the purpose and innate value they contribute. Inspire them by focusing on where they are headed—toward progress and helping others. Through good feelings, inspiration springs forward, so highlight opportunities, possibilities, and team strength. Help your team focus on what they want by getting good feelings out ahead of their day.

4   **Turn problems into solutions.** Remember, the longer your team struggles with problems, the worse they will feel. Help your team move forward by looking at where they want to go, not where they are. Whenever you see behaviors you don't like, try to focus instead on behaviors that you do like. Lift the problem label and focus on opportunities.

5   **Stay connected to bigger goals by celebrating small wins.** Take time to bliss out on appreciation, like when a customer compliments your team. Good feelings tend to spread quickly, so hit refresh throughout the day by celebrating small victories.

10

MANUFACTURE ABUNDANCE

THE LAW OF ATTRACTION IN ACTION

CALEB WAS about five-foot-seven, a bit stocky, and about fifty pounds overweight. Which is why my co-workers and I almost fell over when he introduced us to his wife, a six-foot redhead with a perfect figure.

She was drop-dead gorgeous. When the couple walked away, we all looked at each other and said, "How did he land her?"

The truth is, if you spent five minutes with Caleb and his wife, you could see what was going on. They had love for each other and lots of it. It was unconditional and rare. She wasn't attracted to him by looks or money or dental benefits. She was with him for their shared affection.

If your love for someone is hinged on finances, appearance, or any sort of external perks, you'll always be vulnerable and irritated. These are all conditions that can change. But even worse, your focus on them separates you from your own happiness. Labeling conditions and deficiencies in your partner makes those challenges grow stronger.

The law of attraction says you will attract into your life whatever you focus on. What you think about most becomes your reality.

This means your thoughts and emotions influence your life. Negative thoughts, worry, fear, and doubt make you cautious and hold you back. Positive thoughts encourage you to move forward.

If your life feels like a bunch of fits and starts, look to how you're thinking about it. Things may feel out of your control until you discover how to guide your mental energy toward your dreams.

Vibration

By practicing the feel-good habits in this book, you will start to sense a distinct vibration inside you. Everything vibrates to a particular frequency, including you. Even what appears to be solid is just a collection of tiny moving particles with space between them.

Our thoughts and feelings vibrate in the cells of our body. What seems like a random thought is actually a vibrational energy. Your attention to a thought makes it grow. When similar-feeling thoughts collect and build momentum, they become a powerful point of attraction. This means you naturally attract more thoughts and experiences just like it.

Everything you think about creates your reality. Since this is so, you may as well give your thoughts some direction. You would never plan a vacation without deciding where you're going. However you may be letting your life creep forward without guidance.

If you continually regurgitate thoughts of doubt and fear, more of this will land splat in the middle of your life. The subconscious mind has no sense of humor. It takes every thought as fact. If you could steer those thoughts in the direction of what you want, your life would improve greatly.

It takes practice, but you can choose your dominant vibration through your thoughts.

Lift your vibration

Sustaining positive-feeling thoughts for a longer period of time will cause the cells of your body to vibrate at a higher frequency. The more in alignment you are with positive frequencies, the more you will attract more positive thoughts and things to you.

This is the law of attraction. These are the feel-good habits we have been practicing.

Paying attention to how you feel is the best way to know your vibration, and elevating your thoughts is the best way to create the life you want. If you focus on what you don't want, this will likely produce gloomy thoughts and substandard experiences. But what if you elevate and lift your vibration?

You can manufacture abundance in your life through your thoughts.

Emotional range

Your thoughts and feelings always want to go in the same direction (forward), and trying to pretend they are synchronized when they're not doesn't work.

If you feel angry and tell yourself you're happy, you won't be kidding anyone, including yourself. The frequency of anger is much lower than happiness, so they can't run in the same direction. However, some lower-frequency feelings are closer to happiness than anger, and tapping into them can gradually nudge you toward higher-level feelings. This is developing emotional range.

In the beginning, jumping from a place like grief or fear directly into joy and love may be too ambitious. It might feel like covering up and trying to banish a low state. You could become angry that you're not positive enough.

The law of attraction says **you will attract into your life whatever you focus on.**

So, if you try to feel good, yet your thoughts and emotions gravitate to worry or doubt, thank those feelings for their reappearance. They are giving you information. You are not ready to let go. That's okay. You may just need more time and persistence.

Remember, happiness is a feeling, not a goal. Don't work at it. Just feel a bit better, and then a bit better and then a bit better. Be gentle with yourself.

When you are under stress, you probably don't think clearly. Your logical mind, the prefrontal cortex, is taken over by the emotional part of the brain, at the back, called the hypothalamus. Soothing this reaction takes practice. The most accessible tool you have is your breath. Feeling angry, hurt, upset? Breathe in and out several times and watch the breath. Soothing your emotional brain and climbing toward higher vibration emotions will be a lot easier when your breath is slow and deep.

The emotional vibration scale

I learned about the Emotional Guidance Scale from Esther and Jerry Hicks in their book, *Ask and It Is Given*.[7] The principle is that by focusing on a word/quality for seventeen seconds, you activate a matching vibration. As that vibration becomes stronger, the law of attraction will bring you more thoughts that match. The power of the vibration will expand its reach as you increase your focus on it. The scale helps you choose better-feeling emotions to gradually lift your vibration. The scale is a list of commonly felt emotions ranging from joy and love (the highest) to grief and anger (the lowest). To lift your vibration and feel better, determine where you are on the scale and proactively reach for better-feeling thoughts and emotions.

Experiment with the Emotional Guidance Scale on page 210, using it to gravitate toward higher-vibration thoughts. Use your thoughts to guide you and pay attention to good feelings. In the

EMOTIONAL GUIDANCE SCALE

HIGH VIBRATION

1 Joy · Appreciation · Empowered · Freedom · Love

2 Passion

3 Enthusiasm/Eagerness/Happiness

4 Positive Expectation/Belief

5 Optimism

6 Hopefulness

7 Contentment

8 Boredom

9 Pessimism

10 Frustration/Irritation/Impatience

11 Overwhelmed

12 Disappointment

13 Doubt

14 Worry

15 Blame

16 Discouragement

17 Anger

18 Revenge

19 Hatred/Rage

20 Jealousy

21 Insecurity · Guilt · Unworthiness

22 Fear · Grief · Desperation · Powerlessness

LOW VIBRATION

beginning, don't try to take huge leaps from anger to joy. You likely don't have the emotional range, but it can be developed. For most people, it will be very hard to jump from jealousy to love; it will be a lot easier to elevate from jealousy to rage. Just take yourself lightly in this. You can't get it wrong.

What's the benefit of this? Let's say you feel rage because you discover your spouse lied to you about something important. If you can massage your thoughts to revenge, anger, and then blame—you may move from thoughts of wanting to hurt them to thinking they are unforgivable for what they have done—you have improved your emotional vibration. It may seem odd to think moving from rage to blame is an improvement, but it is. You will know because you will feel a bit better, a slight relief. It is a subtle shift, but it's easier and more realistic than a leap from anger to joy.

Here's an example of moving upward toward higher vibration thoughts. When I'm at the airport waiting for a flight and it gets delayed, I feel immediate doubt and worry that I will miss my event the next morning and lose a lot of money. The longer I chase thoughts of worry and doom around in my brain, the worse I feel. When I catch myself in this cycle, I actively look for a higher vibration thought that offers me relief. If I can just move my thoughts up the scale from worry to being irritated or frustrated with the situation or the airline, this will help. Soon, I can vibrate up toward a bit of hope that there's opportunity in the situation. Eventually, I'll have more optimism and belief that everything will work out.

These are small steps, using the scale above to nudge me toward a higher vibration. Notice that the circumstances (a delayed flight) don't change, but my vibration does. This is all you focus on. Because I've practiced higher vibrations, there are times when I can totally bliss out in happiness when everything around me is falling apart. I will stay focused and see opportunities while many other people are stuck.

Have fun with this scale. If you can tease worry into doubt, you have elevated. If you've ever forced yourself to be happy when you feel anger, you know how hard that is. It doesn't work. When you're in a negative place, high-vibration thoughts won't resonate. You cannot bliss out in joy when you're feeling guilt and unworthiness. Instead, you move slowly up to a higher vibration thought.

As someone with anxiety, I used to find myself experiencing frustration, irritation, and impatience fairly often. Moving those feelings to pessimism and boredom was fairly easy. I focused on boredom for seventeen seconds, and, as if by magic, I felt bored. Hooray for boredom! From boredom, contentment wasn't so far away—seventeen more seconds, and I was in the positive emotions range.

Blissing out with the scale

You can bliss out anywhere within the positive range of the emotional scale. Once you pass contentment, you will feel positive vibrations gain velocity and more easily expand. Choose anything above contentment and bliss out on it for as long as you can. Just sit and marinate in the good vibes your positive thoughts are producing. Sustain this blissed-out feeling for seventeen seconds. Pretty soon, you'll be zipping your way up the scale toward joy. To bliss out, you need to be absorbed in the present moment and let all tension or doubt go. It will help to take a few deep breaths to center yourself.

Once you elevate to the positive emotional thought range, notice your vibration. You will feel lighter, better flowing energy in you. This is good—you are priming yourself to bliss out. Positive emotions are fun, easy, and flowing. You can quite easily glide up the scale from hopefulness to happiness.

Just like a singer increases their vocal range, with practice, you will eventually improve your emotional range. Along the way, whenever you feel stuck, always return to kindness and self-compassion to move your emotions forward.

Have faith in yourself. Over time, this won't be your last-ditch effort to feel good. You will build a more flexible emotional range and regularly dance up and down the emotional scale. Have fun with it. Pretty soon you will notice you can gracefully glide from discouragement to joy with no residual doubt holding you back.

· · · FEEL-GOOD HABITS · · ·

1 **Study the law of attraction.** If you want more information on the law of attraction, go immediately to any content
developed by Abraham, Esther, or Jerry Hicks. They are some
of the original and best sources of information about the
power of attraction.

2 **Pay attention to what are you manifesting.** The law of
attraction will only give you what you are ready for. You can
look at your life right now and see the vibrational quality of
your thoughts and what they are producing. When something
unfavorable happens, know that your thoughts helped create
those circumstances. Take a brief look at your life, things
you like and things you don't, and see if you can glimpse the
thoughts behind the life you have created. Remember, you
are one thought away from change, so determine what you
want, if you decide you want to change your life.

3 **Write a "future you" journal.** Imagine yourself next year.
What do you want your future to look like? Write about it and
how great it will feel. Notice those elated feelings in you in
the now, as you write.

4 **Live "as if it is."** Start living as if your desired reality already
is true. For instance, buy clothes you would wear on the first
day of your dream job. Or go shopping for your dream house;
even if you can't afford it, just browse but imagine you live
there. It's the vibrational feeling this dreaming gives you that
matters. Bliss out on that feeling.

5 **Let it go.** When you obsess or worry about what isn't working, you attract more of what you don't want. Release these thoughts and relax. It may help to have fun and think about something else for a while. Ask yourself what you want instead.

11

FINE-TUNE YOUR AWARENESS

MINDFULNESS LIFTS THE HUSTLE

WHEN I travel, I miss my son, Branden. So I start to imagine all the great things we will do together. By the time I get home, I've made very detailed plans for our time together. I'll squeeze in the zoo, the science center, even a movie—all in one day.

But sometimes I'm so busy tracking our time and rushing us to the next venue, I realize I'm missing the moments. Precious moments—the sly glance Branden gives me when he's being mischievous, the pure joy and delight he has when playing in the sandbox, or the love I feel when I hold his hand—can be small and easy to brush off.

Such moments come alive not in the doing, but in the feeling. If we're not being mindful, we miss them. We can be busy *doing* all day long, but it's our feelings that make things matter.

To nourish your feelings, you need to be mindful of them. The act of mindfully paying attention to good feelings erupting in your chest and flowing through your body can open up the floodgates for more positive emotions.

If you have been doing the activities in this book, you have been practicing forms of mindfulness. *Mindfulness* means focusing on what you're sensing and feeling in the moment, without interpretation or judgment. I've been encouraging you to focus on your good feelings, noticing them without manipulating them. Blissing out is being mindful of good feelings in your body.

Being versus doing

Do you find it difficult to stay focused on what's happening at the moment? Do you rush through chores without really paying attention to them? Are you often preoccupied with your thoughts?

Mindfulness sees life unfold moment by moment, unencumbered by skepticism and doubt. The more you focus on good feelings, the more accepting and mindful you are.

You can't control what life throws at you, but you can adjust your perspective. Mindfulness trains you to do this. It helps you pause and control your responses in stressful situations. You can notice a jumble of conflicting emotions inside you in a calm and detached manner. You can savor the beauty that is always available in the life right in front of you.

If mindfulness has a destination, it's to bring you into your life now. Mindfulness pays attention to what is happening while it is happening. It employs kind curiosity rather than judgment. In a split second, mindfulness can pull you out of thoughts that transport you into the past or future and plant your attention into the now.

As we've already explored, our predominant thought patterns are usually negative. They release adrenaline and cortisol, and over time can damage our health and well-being. Mindfulness practices can put a stop to your regurgitation of doubt and drama all over your future.

Mindfulness cultivates curiosity and openness. It helps you drop attachment to outcomes and habitual small-minded thoughts. It temporarily lifts the burden of stress. Instead of remembering torturous events of the past, you pay attention to the moment you're in and accept it.

Your body is talking to you all the time, giving you clues to what's going on inside you. It doesn't yell at you like missing a goal does. It is subtler. The more urgently it needs you to hear it, the louder it gets. For example, painful migraine headaches are your body trying to tell you something—likely to slow down and pay attention to it.

To bliss out is to be mindful

When you bliss out and sustain a positive vibration, you are mindfully paying attention to the good feeling inside you. This means you are focused in the here and now and curiously exploring feelings of joyful bliss.

When you bliss out, you are fully absorbed in the present moment.

Lift your gaze from this page. Put a light attention on your breath. In and out. Notice the feeling of calm wash over you. There, you were just mindful. You can dip into mindfulness anytime you have a couple seconds. In the same way you paid attention to your breath, you can be mindful of your good-feeling emotions.

Meditation is a common mindfulness practice. It quiets your mind and helps you pay attention to your body, often by focusing on the breath. However, there are many ways to be mindful. The best way to understand mindfulness is to dive right in.

The tease-apart method

The tease-apart method to mindfulness is a quick way to corral your wild mind from darting around. It creates instant focus

When you bliss out, **you are fully absorbed in the present moment.**

and calm. Anytime you focus on your environment using any of your senses, you locate the present moment. You use your senses to guide you to the now.

Stop and choose one of your senses—sound, smell, taste, sight, or touch. Now focus on that sense and tease apart nuances within it.

Sound. What can you hear in your environment right now? Search for a sound, once you isolate it, focus on that sound for a second, notice its texture and quality, and let it go. Now listen for another distinct sound; as soon as you hear it, focus on it for a moment and let it go. Move on to the next sound. Tease apart sound, and you will notice some sounds vibrate as a low hum while others are a louder roar.

Smell. Can you tease apart a couple of smells right now? How about coffee, body odor, or perfume? Notice each one for a second and move on to the next.

Taste. Bite into a hamburger and tease apart the doughy bun, notice the grease leaking out of the ground beef. Appreciate the bursts of pepper squeezed in that jump at your pallet.

Sight. Choose anything in your environment and notice its color, shape, and size. Let that image go and move on to something else. You can lightly focus on the floor, the ceiling, the lights, the decor. You are not judging what you see; you are noticing it.

Touch. Grasp hold of something near you—for example, the armrest of a chair. Notice its gritty, worn texture, notice if it is warm or cool to the skin. Now let go of the chair and reach for something else with the same kind of mindful awareness.

This technique uses your senses, connected to your feelings, to pull your attention into the present moment. Each one of your senses is interpreting a vibration. Latch on to one of your senses at any time to navigate to the now.

You can bring this mindfulness to the daily hustle and bustle of your life, too, to be mindful throughout the day, not just when it's convenient. There are simple things you can do, unnotice-able by others, to find calm. Simply watch your breath or tune in to your senses. Do this standing in line at Costco, in a business meeting, or while driving to work.

While you are walking, notice your feet hit the ground. Feel your heel all the way to your toes as they contact the sidewalk, the trail, the sand. Does this practice make you walk slower? Do you wobble on high heels, or do they make you align your body and stand up taller? What does the earth feel like under your bare feet?

When you notice the simple things in life, you are learning the art of appreciation. Soon it will unfold and flower into all corners. When you notice something, resist the temptation to label or judge it. Just be curious about it and let it go.

Mindfulness is an attitude as well as a practice. It offers you spaciousness and perspective. Focusing mindfully on something without judging it trains your mind to release attachment to outcomes. It helps you stay focused, present, and non-critical.

Instant mindfulness: focus on the breath

The most common way to learn to focus your attention is by focusing on the breath. By watching your breath, you train your brain to slow down and concentrate on just one thing. Your breath is a natural target that grounds you in the here and now, in your life.

There are three things you need to know about breath and how it supports mindfulness.

First, it is the path of least resistance. Hey, diligent, driven person! Something you do happens without your input or effort.

Unlike other areas of your life, it doesn't need goals and spread-sheets to matter. It doesn't rely on you, scold you, or need you to perform. You can neglect it for decades, and it will still do its thing. It's keeping you alive. It's your breath.

It may be relieving to know that you can't mess this up. You also don't have to work at it.

Second, breath anchors you in the present. To feel good and move forward, you can train the mind to give way to the present moment. You may find it easy to focus on the single thing that is always with you: your breath. Several times a day, relish in a few deep breaths. Blend your inside world with the outside world with grace and ease. Breath anchors your attention in your body and in the moment. Your body is your friend, and your breath will help you get acquainted.

Third, breath takes your internal emotional temperature. If you are open to it, your breath will give you some clues to your life. It can be your thermometer, taking your temperature, tell-ing you to slow down. Shallow-chest breathing is instigated by stress. Anxiety, worry, and fear restrict breathing. Is your breath deep or shallow? Rough or smooth? Being a try-hard personality, you will likely try to manipulate the breath and deepen its flow. Turn that ambition toward the practice of sim-ply observing. Notice how, when you breathe, your muscles tend to naturally loosen their grip and relax.

Meditation

You've probably guessed that this book is based around princi-ples of mindfulness. I have been an avid meditator for more than twenty years. I never endure a day without meditation. It helps me quiet myself and tune in.

The practice of slowing down and watching your breath is meditation. And there are so many other types, including chakras, pure awareness, guided imagery, yoga nidra, kundalini, and mindfulness. Here, Google and YouTube are your friends. We are so fortunate to have so many quality free meditation videos and guides floating around the Internet. I recommend you experiment, adopt a mediation you like, and practice it regularly. (You will find some basic instructions for a couple of methods of meditation in the "Feel-good habits" section of this chapter and more on my YouTube channel.)

Something to know about meditation practices: They are all good. Some are just quieter than others. A noisy meditation is the result of a busy mind that relentlessly won't let go of thoughts. If you notice thoughts keep commandeering your attention and sweep you out of awareness, you have a noisy mind.

Every time you lasso your attention and bring your mind back to the present moment, you improve your power of observation. You may notice there is a tight mental fist wrapped around restless thoughts or specific body pains. Climb right into those thoughts and that body pain and bring kindness to them, along with curious attention without judgment. If you can fully accept your pains, they will lose their grip on your insides.

Noisy meditation is more challenging, but I sense it creates deeper change because it takes effort to keep bringing the brain back and settling your thoughts. Like building muscles, you are developing focus and awareness every time you bring the mind back to sensing.

One of my favorite types of meditation is metta, which cultivates a propensity for kindness. As a success-driven individual, you need to squeeze kindness onto your to-do list. I recommend carving out time to say nice things to yourself and think nice thoughts about others. If you do it while focusing on your breath, the words will marinate in your subconscious mind and will integrate more easily into your life.

Meditation can help your relationship with your body. Your body is your vessel. Whether you approve of its size or shape, it's yours and it's the only one you get. Take care of it. Also build a relationship with it. Inhabit it, understand its nuisances, aches, and pains—usually they are telling you something.

A body scan meditation quiets your mind as you spend time gently tootling around inside your body. Slowly you audit any discomfort, muscle aches, and restlessness. When you stumble on pain or distraction you breathe into it. Never judging or analyzing, just soaking it in and accepting it. You open the door to pain or discomfort and tune in to the messages your body is sending.

To stick with my theme of repetition in this book, I will review how to mindfully bliss out: Breath in and out several times to release any tension.

Use any pleasing thought to call up good feelings in your body (positive affirmation, appreciating something, thinking about someone you love, visualization). Focus on good feelings in your body and notice them expand as you focus on them. Notice how your vibration keeps rising. Bliss out on these good feelings.

Halt the hustle

I hope you have found inspiration through these pages. I'd love for you to rely on happiness as a force more powerful than hustle. Never again do you have to ramp up your effort to achieve things. Instead, you can let happiness propel you toward what you desire. Before you act, always align with your good feelings.

Bliss out often in your good vibes.

To end this book, I want to give you a short motivational speech and leave you with my favorite poem. I hope that you now feel a good vibrational wind beneath your wings and are moving forward.

The real purpose of your life is to feel good living it.

Never give up on your dreams

Boldly go in the direction of your dreams.

Stand tall and show the world your passion. When the world beats you down, find a reason to get back up again. Never give up on feeling good. Keep moving forward.

Turbo charge your life with positive energy. It will propel you forward.

This is your beautiful life. Live it.

Feed your mind ideas of success, not failure.

Remember, the only way you can fail is if you give up. Every time you fail, you come one step closer to success.

Tell your brain what you want rather than what you don't want. Label your powerful life in an almighty way.

You are not scared; you are kind and courageous. You are not weak; you are powerful. You are not ordinary; you are remarkable.

Do not back down, do not give up.

When you look back on your life, don't have regrets. Believe in yourself, believe in your future, you will find your way.

There is a passion burning inside you that is very powerful; it is waiting to burn bright. You are meant to do great things.

Courage is facing fear with compassion. Fear of failure holds most people back, but you are not most people.

Most people master the obvious; you are creating something that wasn't there before. It's bold, it's beautiful, and it's you.

Give it your best, and your dreams will come to life. Success is yours.

Go for your dreams; it is your turn.

If mindfulness
has a destination,
**it's to bring
you into your
life now.**

The reward is within

The contest lasts for moments
Though the training's taken years,
It wasn't the winning alone that
Was worth the work and the tears
The applause will be forgotten
The prize will be misplaced
But the long hard hours of practice
Will never be a waste
For in trying to win
You build a skill
You learn that winning
Depends on will
You never grow by how much you win
You only grow by how much you put in
So any new challenge
You've just begun
Put forth your best
And you've already won.

BILL CLENNAN inspirational speaker,
and the most inspiring person I've ever known

· · · FEEL-GOOD HABITS · · ·

1   **Do a basic breath meditation.** Close your eyes. Sit comfort-
ably with your feet flat on the floor and your spine straight,
or you may choose to lie down. Relax your whole body. Keep
your eyes closed and bring your awareness inward. Without
straining or concentrating, just relax. Take a deep breath in.
And breathe out.

   When thoughts pop up, notice them, and let them go.
Refocus on your breath. You might guide your awareness to
any tension in your body to release it. Focus on your breath.
Do this for as long as you can.

2   **Do a body scan meditation.** Close your eyes. Take a few deep
breaths and let them relax you and quiet your mind. Bring
nonjudgmental awareness to your feet and work your way
up your body. Scan through each section of your body, gently
shining a spotlight on different areas. Hang out in different
parts of your body for as long as you like. Let your mind steer
your attention while playing a background role to sensing
and feeling. You're building a stronger mind-body connection.

   Be patient. Countless networks in your brain are rewiring
as you do this. Some parts of your body will speak louder
than others. Don't attempt to label or judge any feelings.
Just bring acceptance and awareness to yourself and anything that comes up as you pay attention.

   Check out my YouTube channel for free guided meditations.

Notes

1   Mindful Staff. "Jon Kabat-Zinn: Defining Mindfulness," Mindful, January 11, 2017, mindful.org/jon-kabat-zinn-defining-mindfulness/

2   Abraham Hicks, abraham-hicks.com

3   Alan S. Cowen and Dacher Keltner. "Self-Report Captures 27 Distinct Categories of Emotion Bridged by Continuous Gradients," *Proceedings of the National Academy of Sciences 114*: 38 (September 2017): E7900–E7909, pnas.org/content/114/38/E7900

4   David Cox. "Everything You Ever Wanted to Know about Hangovers (but Were Too Queasy to Ask)," *The Guardian*, December 12, 2016, theguardian .com/lifeandstyle/2016/dec/12/everything-you-wanted-to-know-about-hangovers

5   Mindful Staff. "What You Practice Grows Stronger," Mindful, March 24, 2017, mindful.org/practice-grows-stronger

6   Prakhar Verma. "Destroy Negativity from Your Mind with This Simple Exercise," Mission.org, November 27, 2017, medium.com/the-mission/a-practical-hack-to-combat-negative-thoughts-in-2-minutes-or-less-cc3d1bddb3af

7   Esther and Jerry Hicks. *Ask and It Is Given: Learning to Manifest Your Desires* (Carlsbad, CA: Hay House, 2004).

Further Reading

Books on Happiness

If you crave more nitty-gritty research on happiness, I suggest you dig into any of the following books.

***The Art of Happiness: A Handbook for Living* by His Holiness the Dalai Lama and Howard C. Cutler, MD**
Written by a psychiatrist, based on interviews with the Dalai Lama, the book suggests happiness is the purpose of life and anyone can be happy.

***Authentic Happiness: Using the New Positive Psychology to Realize Your Potential for Lasting Fulfillment* by Martin E.P. Seligman, PhD**
Written by the doctor known as the father of modern psychology, this book suggests focusing on your strengths to improve your life and includes checklists and theories to assess your happiness.

*The Happiness Advantage: How a Positive Brain
Fuels Success in Work and Life* by **Shawn Achor**
Shawn Achor, a lecturer at Harvard, conducted the largest ever study on happiness. He reveals the seven core principles of positive psychology that people can use to enhance their performance and improve their career.

*The Happiness Trap: How to Stop Struggling
and Start Living* by **Russ Harris**
The main argument of this book is that the more people try to achieve happiness the further away they will be from it. Dr. Harris recommends the ACT (Acceptance and Commitment Therapy) technique based on mindfulness to bring happiness into you in the moment.

Books on Mindfulness and Spirituality

*Mindfulness: An Eight-Week Plan for Finding Peace in a
Frantic World* by **Mark Williams** and **Danny Penman**
Based on the techniques of Mindfulness-Based Cognitive Therapy, this book offers a unique program of simple and straightforward forms of mindfulness meditation. I took the course online, and I found it very valuable.

*The Power of Now: A Guide to Spiritual
Enlightenment* by **Eckhart Tolle**
Eckhart Tolle shows us how to leave behind our ego and analytical mind to bring us into the now. Tolle reinforces how problems do not exist in the present moment. This book contains some powerful keys to enter into a state of inner peace.

*The Untethered Soul: The Journey
Beyond Yourself* by **Michael A. Singer**
Loaded with insight on letting go of negative thoughts and being
in the present moment, this book aims to turn your attention
inward to discover your true inner voice. Becoming untethered
is not so much about learning a skill as it is about rediscover-
ing yourself.

Books on Compassion

*Radical Compassion: Learning to Love Yourself and
Your World with the Practice of RAIN* by **Tara Brach**
RAIN is a four-step meditation that helps you release your grip
on difficult emotions and limiting beliefs. Discover step-by-step
how to let go of loss and suffering. Tara Brach is one of the most
trusted mindfulness teachers in America.

*Self-Compassion: The Proven Power of
Being Kind to Yourself* by **Kristin Neff, PhD**
Dr. Neff turns the emphasis away from self-esteem and toward
self-compassion. This book helps you limit self-criticism with
self-kindness and offers exercises for dealing with struggle
with compassion.

Books on the Law of Attraction

*Ask and It Is Given: Learning to Manifest
Your Desires* by **Esther and Jerry Hicks**
Esther and Jerry Hicks (Abraham Hicks Publications) have written some of the most inspiring and relatable books on the law
of attraction. The Hicks's Law of Attraction says people create

their own reality through their attention and focus. Emotions are a person's guidance system that indicates how close or distant that person is to how their source feels about a particular topic of focus.

Based on the Teachings of Abraham—also the central source of inspiration to Rhonda Byrnes's *The Secret*—*Ask and It Is Given* is a great introduction to the Law of Attraction, showing readers how to turn their attention away from problems and stress and ask for what they want instead. This uplifting guide shows that life is meant to be fun and easy.

I highly recommend watching a few YouTube videos of Esther Hicks. Simply search her name, and you will find hundreds of videos.

Infinite Possibilities: The Art of Living Your Dreams by Mike Dooley

An uplifting book to help you understand the power you have to transform your beliefs and attract a better life.

The Success Principles: How to Get from Where You Are to Where You Want to Be by Jack Canfield

A straightforward guide to learning how to increase confidence, overcome challenges, live with purpose, and manifest your ambitions.

Think and Grow Rich by Napoleon Hill

Napoleon Hill uses stories of some of the most famous millionaires from his generation to illustrate the power of the law of attraction.

Wealth Beyond Reason: Mastering
the Law of Attraction by Bob Doyle
This book combines science and the law of attraction to show you how to create a life of abundance. Anyone skeptical of the law of attraction should consider this book.

About the Author

F ED UP with living a mediocre life, Jody decided she wanted a memorable one instead. Her unyielding ambition fueled her into the crazy world of stand-up comedy, a place where she learned to roll with the punchlines and turn life's lemons into a delicious lemonade. She is also a motivational speaker and participates in more than one hundred events per year.

Her mission is simple: to eagerly empower worn-out professionals with humor, hindsight, and hallelujahs. With more than twenty-three years of experience inspiring and entertaining over a hundred audiences per year across the globe, Jody Urquhart delivers uplifting, engaging motivational speeches that help professionals cultivate a much-needed blissful can-do attitude toward fun and meaningful work.

Every keynote she delivers is a stepping stone toward her audiences building the life they have always wanted.

She is the author of the book *All Work & No Say*, a tongue-in-cheek insight into the rat race and how to find joy.

Jody uses the law of attraction in her everyday life, which has amplified her career and helped her create a blissful life. In her spare time she loves to meditate and still performs stand-up comedy, but not at the same time.

Connect with Jody!

WANT MORE to bliss out on? Visit Jody Urquhart's website for ways to connect with her through her speaking, her blog, and her newsletter. We have also created free, downloadable recordings exclusively for you:

- Bliss out on daily feel-good habits on Instagram—follow @jody_urquhart

- Get Your Bliss On—a ten-minute morning inspiration boost

- Manifesting the Life You Want—a ten-minute meditation and visualization to create the life you're dreaming of

- Bliss Out for Prosperity—fifty affirmations for health, wealth, and happiness

- Bliss Out for Relaxation—a ten-minute meditation for relaxation

- Don't Be So Hard on Yourself—a ten-minute self-kindness meditation

blissoutbook.com

Bliss Out with Your Team

BY NOW, you probably feel some steady bliss but want your colleagues to join you in creating an uplifting work environment.

Here are some ways to bring *Bliss Out* to your team:

Copies for Your Whole Team

Buy copies of *Bliss Out* for your whole team, and I will send you our 100 Feel-Good Habits PDF or PowerPoint that you can use to spread your bliss. We also have several inspirational video formats to share with your team.

Contact me for bulk discounts and special offers. We can also do custom additions that can include a personalized message from your CEO. Just shoot us an email at jody@idoinspire.com.

Speaking at Your Event

Need a little more inspiration to keep rejuvenating your team bliss? You plan the event, and I'll do a 60- to 90-minute keynote talk. Bring *Bliss Out* inspiration into your organization either virtually or in person.

CPSIA information can be obtained
at www.ICGtesting.com
Printed in the USA
BVHW030221060122
624564BV00001B/53